D1627140

Jennifer Aniston

Jennifer Aniston

by Rachel Lynette

LUCENT BOOKS
A part of Gale, Cengage Learning

GALE
CENGAGE Learning™

Detroit • New York • San Francisco • New Haven, Conn • Waterville, Maine • London

GALE
CENGAGE Learning™

For Lucy, who knows how to be a good friend

LIBRARY OF CONGRESS CATALOGING-IN-PUBLICATION DATA

Lynette, Rachel.
  Jennifer Aniston / by Rachel Lynette.
    p. cm. -- (People in the news)
  Includes bibliographical references and index.
  ISBN 978-1-4205-0235-0 (hardcover)
  1. Aniston, Jennifer--Juvenile literature. 2. Actors--United States--Biography--Juvenile literature. I. Title.
  PN2287.A62L96 2010
  791.4502'8092--dc22
  [B]
                                                        2009040310

Lucent Books
27500 Drake Rd.
Farmington Hills, MI 48331

ISBN-13: 978-1-4205-0235-0
ISBN-10: 1-4205-0235-2

Printed in the United States of America
 2 3 4 5 6 7 13 12 11 10

Printed by Bang Printing, Brainerd, MN, 2ⁿᵈ Ptg., 07/2010

Contents

F ame and celebrity are alluring. People are drawn to those who walk in fame's spotlight, whether they are known for great accomplishments or for notorious deeds. The lives of the famous pique public interest and attract attention, perhaps because their experiences seem in some ways so different from, yet in other ways so similar to, our own.

Newspapers, magazines, and television regularly capitalize on this fascination with celebrity by running profiles of famous people. For example, television programs such as *Entertainment Tonight* devote all of their programming to stories about entertainment and entertainers. Magazines such as *People* fill their pages with stories of the private lives of famous people. Even newspapers, newsmagazines, and television news frequently delve into the lives of well-known personalities. Despite the number of articles and programs, few provide more than a superficial glimpse at their subjects.

Lucent's People in the News series offers young readers a deeper look into the lives of today's newsmakers, the influences that have shaped them, and the impact they have had in their fields of endeavor and on other people's lives. The subjects of the series hail from many disciplines and walks of life. They include authors, musicians, athletes, political leaders, entertainers, entrepreneurs, and others who have made a mark on modern life and who, in many cases, will continue to do so for years to come.

These biographies are more than factual chronicles. Each book emphasizes the contributions, accomplishments, or deeds that have brought fame or notoriety to the individual and shows how that person has influenced modern life. Authors portray their subjects in a realistic, unsentimental light. For example, Bill Gates—the cofounder and chief executive officer of the software giant Microsoft—has been instrumental in making personal computers the most vital tool of the modern age. Few dispute his business savvy, his perseverance, or his technical expertise, yet critics say he is ruthless in his dealings with competitors and driven more by his desire to maintain Microsoft's dominance in the computer industry than by an interest in furthering technology.

In these books, young readers will encounter inspiring stories about real people who achieved success despite enormous obstacles. Oprah Winfrey—the most powerful, most watched, and wealthiest woman on television today—spent the first six years of her life in the care of her grandparents while her unwed mother sought work and a better life elsewhere. Her adolescence was colored by promiscuity, pregnancy at age fourteen, rape, and sexual abuse.

Each author documents and supports his or her work with an array of primary and secondary source quotations taken from diaries, letters, speeches, and interviews. All quotes are footnoted to show readers exactly how and where biographers derive their information and provide guidance for further research. The quotations enliven the text by giving readers eyewitness views of the life and accomplishments of each person covered in the People in the News series.

In addition, each book in the series includes photographs, annotated bibliographies, timelines, and comprehensive indexes. For both the casual reader and the student researcher, the People in the News series offers insight into the lives of today's newsmakers—people who shape the way we live, work, and play in the modern age.

Everyone's Favorite Friend

Jennifer Aniston is best known for her role as Rachel Green on the hugely popular sitcom *Friends*. For ten years millions of viewers followed the lives of the six friends as they coped with relationships, careers, and even babies. *Friends* was the show that everyone watched on Thursday night and everyone talked about on Friday morning. Although there were six friends, Rachel, with her perfectly toned body, perky personality, and sought-after haircut, was often the favorite. Her on-again, off-again relationship with the goofy but lovable Ross kept audiences coming back week after week. Viewers fell in love not only with the character she played, but with Aniston herself. Aniston's warm and open personality, along with her quick wit and ready smile, made her popular with both the media and the public. Frequently called "Hollywood's Sweetheart," her face on the cover of a magazine was sure to result in extra sales.

Aniston was not only popular with the public, but also with her costars on *Friends*. The six cast members forged real-life friendships, not unlike the ones they portrayed on the show. All six of them stuck together through their rise to fame, challenges with the media, and even contract negotiations with the studio. Although the entire cast of *Friends* was close, Aniston forged a special relationship with costar Courteney Cox. In addition to Cox, Aniston has several lifelong friends who have helped her through difficult times in both childhood and her adult life. Aniston has said many times that her friends are her family.

Aniston began relying on her friends early in life because she could not always rely on her parents, who divorced when she was nine. Aniston did not see much of her father, soap opera star John Aniston, after the divorce. Aniston's mother, Nancy Dow, harbored bitterness over the divorce, which often spilled into her parenting. As a single mother she had difficulty letting her daughter live her own life and was often critical of her appearance and her friends. Aniston stopped speaking to her mother in 1996 when Dow publicly criticized her daughter, first on a TV talk show and then in a tell-all memoir.

Due to their estrangement, Aniston's mother was not invited to witness her daughter's marriage to superstar Brad Pitt in a million-dollar wedding ceremony in July 2000. Called "Hollywood's Golden Couple," the pair was adored by the public. The two appeared to be blissfully in love and were thought to be the ideal couple. Pitt was romantic and affectionate toward his wife, and Aniston often talked about how Pitt was her best friend. However, the marriage lasted only five years.

Friends and fans rallied behind Aniston when the couple divorced in 2005 amid rumors of an affair between Pitt and actor Angelina Jolie. Aniston was grateful for the support of her friends, but not so welcome in her life were the paparazzi, which followed her around constantly. Daily, details of her personal life were front-page news on a variety of tabloids. Often the headlines were not even true. Aniston not only had to deal with the heartbreak of her broken marriage, but also with the humiliation of having it shared with the entire world.

Although her personal life was in turmoil, Aniston was successfully making the jump from TV to movies. At first, Aniston played it safe, choosing romantic comedies and roles that were not that different from Rachel on *Friends*. However, as her confidence on the big screen grew, she began to take on more challenging roles. Although many of her movies got mixed or even bad reviews, she has starred in a few critically acclaimed films, such as *The Good Girl* and *Friends with Money*, as well as several box office hits, including *Bruce Almighty*, *The Break-Up*, and *Marley and Me*. Aniston built a reputation as a talented actor who was dedicated to her work and easygoing as well. Costars and directors

Jennifer Aniston is considered one of the world's leading actresses. She achieved success in both television and film and is now turning to producing.

frequently commented that for a big star, Aniston was surprisingly unassuming and down-to-earth.

Now in her forties, Aniston says she is in the best shape of her life, and many of her fans say she looks better than ever. Although she has not yet achieved her lifelong dream of having children, Aniston is thrilled with the life she is living and excited about the future. Having established herself as one of the world's leading actresses, Aniston is turning to producing. Along with friend Kristin Hahn, Aniston founded Echo Films, which focuses on producing movies based on real-life stories. Echo has several projects in the works, including a musical set in the 1940s. Through her films and her recent interest in producing, Aniston has clearly shown that she can be much more than the "Friend" that jump-started her career.

Chapter 1

A Rocky Beginning

Jennifer Joanne Aniston was born in Sherman Oaks, California, on February 11, 1969. Jennifer spent her first years in a small, run-down bungalow that her parents were slowly renovating. At times the house was so torn up that tarps replaced a wall. Although both her parents were aspiring actors, neither had found stardom, and the young family struggled financially.

In addition to financial problems, her parents also had relationship problems, which they rarely hid from their children. Yelling was common in the Aniston home. At times Jennifer felt like she had to be the adult because her parents were acting like children. Jennifer's relationship with her father was often distant, while her relationship with her mother was so close it was sometimes smothering. However, there were good times, too. Jennifer shared a close relationship with her older half brother and her grandmother. She also made friends easily and always seemed to be part of a large social group.

Acting in the Family

Jennifer's father, John Aniston, was born on the island of Crete in Greece. His family came to the United States when he was ten and settled in Pennsylvania, where they opened a family diner. After graduating from high school, Aniston attended Pennsylvania State University and earned a degree in theater arts. He served in the U.S. Navy before pursuing his acting career.

Jennifer's mother, Nancy Dow, was born in Connecticut. Dow was one of six children, all girls, and the daughter of factory workers. Most of her childhood was spent in poverty and moving frequently. When Dow was twelve, her mother took the youngest child and left the family. Her father raised Dow and her sisters by himself. When she was seventeen, Dow married an older man and had a son, Johnny. Dow filed for divorce when Johnny was two years old.

Soon after her divorce, Nancy Dow met John Aniston. The two dated for three years before marrying in 1965. During this time Dow worked sporadically as a model. In the three years before Jennifer was born, Dow and Aniston both appeared in a smattering of television shows, but for the most part the two aspiring actors did not land many acting jobs. Shortly after Jennifer's birth, Dow decided to give up her career to focus on raising her children.

Little Sister Jenny

Jennifer's half brother, Johnny, was eight years old when she was born. According to their mother, Johnny took his role as big brother seriously and was always eager to help take care of his little sister. "From the beginning he designated himself to be her protector. When we went to play in the park, he made sure that she had plenty of cool water to drink and that the kids didn't throw sand. On outings he was in charge of pointing to everything she needed to see and more. Jen adored her big brother and a great love between them developed,"[1] says Dow.

When Jennifer was two years old, she was baptized in a traditional Greek ceremony. Her godparents were Telly and Lynn Savalas, close family friends. Telly Savalas was a successful actor best known for playing the lead role in the TV police drama *Kojak*. After the ceremony the family rode in the Savalases' Rolls Royce back to their home in Beverly Hills for a celebration. Although little Jennifer's behavior had been angelic during the baptism, on the way to the celebration, she vomited her entire breakfast all over her new godfather, her mother, and the interior of the car. According to family legend, Jennifer's grandmother collected and saved the vomit because it contained holy water.

Although they are eight years apart in age, Jennifer Aniston and her half brother, John Mellick, were very close growing up.

A Family in Trouble

As Jennifer grew older, things became more stressful at home. John Aniston's agent did not renew his contract, and his dreams of acting were fading. He tried selling real estate and insurance but did poorly at both. Frustrated by the lack of money and what she perceived as her husband's laziness, Dow frequently lost her

Godfather and Friend, Telly Savalas

John Aniston first met Telly Savalas years before Jennifer was born, when the two were cast on the same episode of *Combat*, a popular TV show in the 1960s. Already a successful actor, Savalas was the guest star, and Aniston had a much smaller role as "Greek #2." Savalas and Aniston shared a common Greek heritage and soon became best friends.

Jennifer remembers her godfather as kind and generous. For her seventh birthday he gave her a pink bicycle, and he often sent her lollipops from the set of his TV show, *Kojak*. On the show, Savalas played a New York City detective with a fondness for lollipops. Savalas died of cancer in January 1994, just before Aniston landed her role on *Friends*. Aniston attended his funeral.

Telly Savalas, star of Kojak, a CBS crime drama from the 1970s, was Jennifer Aniston's godfather.

temper. Fights between Jennifer's parents were not uncommon. Finally, Aniston decided to pursue a career in medicine.

At forty-one Aniston could not find a medical school in the United States that would accept him. The family decided to go to Greece so that Aniston could study there. They sold their little house and moved to Greece when Jennifer was five years old. However, Aniston was not admitted to medical school in Greece, either. After spending a year touring the country and staying with relatives, the family returned to the United States. With no home of their own, they stayed in Pennsylvania with Jennifer's grandmother, who still occupied the home her son had lived in as a boy.

Aniston's luck changed soon after their return when he landed a part on a popular daytime soap opera, *Love of Life*. The show was filmed in New York, so the family moved to an apartment in Manhattan, where Jennifer attended the Rudolf Steiner School. Jennifer adjusted well to her new life in New York and made many friends at school. "A genuine love for everyone seemed to pour out of Jennifer's calm, easy manner. I never knew anyone who had so many friends and there was usually one or more in our home,"[2] said Dow.

Finally, things seemed to be going well for the Aniston family. There was enough money, and the family enjoyed an active social life, often getting together with other families from Aniston's soap opera. Aniston was even gaining enough fame to be recognized by fans when he was out in public. Jennifer and her brother were happy. Everything changed when Jennifer was just nine years old, however. Her father left her mother for one of his costars. Aniston told the story of how she found out about her parents' separation to *Rolling Stone* reporter Nancy Collins:

> Oh, I was shocked. . . . My mom told me. I went to a birthday party, and when I came back, she said, "Your father's not going to be around here for a little while." She didn't say he was gone forever. I don't know if I blocked it, but I just remember sitting there, crying, not understanding that he was gone. I don't know what I did later that night or the next day. I don't remember anything other than it being odd that all of a sudden my father wasn't there. And he was gone for a while. . . . About a year.[3]

Jennifer did not see her father during that first year, and when she did start to visit him on the weekends, they did not always get along. "It was awful," she says. "I felt so totally responsible. . . . I really felt it was because I wasn't a good enough kid. And then on top of that, my dad wasn't great with kids."[4] Her older brother

When Jennifer Aniston was five years old, her father, John Aniston, moved the family to Greece for a year. The family then settled in New York when John landed a role on a daytime soap opera.

had graduated from high school and left for California a few months earlier, so Jennifer and her mother were on their own. The two lived in an apartment on the twenty-first floor of a housing project. Although it was in a seedy neighborhood, they had a balcony and could see the Empire State Building, which Jennifer loved. Although Jennifer was close to her mother, things did not always go smoothly. Dow tried to make a happy home for Jennifer, but parenting by herself was stressful, and she admits that she often yelled at her daughter. In addition, Dow did not get what she considered to be a fair settlement from the divorce, and money was often tight. Fortunately, Jennifer's father agreed to continue to pay her school tuition.

Rebel with a Cause

Although her home life was traumatic, for a time Jennifer thrived at school. The Steiner school emphasized creativity and artistic pursuits. At nine Jennifer was one of ten students whose work was chosen for a special exhibit at the Metropolitan Museum of Art. At eleven she joined the drama club, where she got some of her first acting instruction. "I joined the drama club and I just loved it. . . . I loved the energy and the fun of being able to play,"[5] said Aniston. One thing that Jennifer did not like about the Steiner school was that it discouraged television. "I'd sneak it all the time, of course," said Aniston. "You become obsessed with anything your parents tell you not to do. Plus, Dad had left. How could I connect with him? He was on the television!"[6]

Adolescence brought changes for what had previously been an imaginative, fun-loving girl. By ninth grade Jennifer's grades were falling, and she lost interest in school. She changed her look by shaving her hair into a kind of Mohawk, using a lot of black eye makeup, wearing a lot of earrings, and dressing only in black. She also began intentionally getting in trouble in an attempt to bring her parents back together. "When I got in trouble, my mom and dad would have to meet at the principal's office. There was that little manipulation for a while. But it didn't work out. It's hard to impress your dad when you're in the principal's office for being stupid,"[7] said Aniston.

Jennifer's Wonderful Gift

By high school Jennifer knew she wanted to be an actor. Although her father loved acting, he discouraged her from following in his footsteps. He worried that she would be hurt by the almost constant rejection and wanted to protect his only daughter from what can be a very cruel profession. Rather than be discouraged by her father's advice, Jennifer felt challenged. "I wanted to prove to him that I could do it. I thought he would then be unbelievably impressed and would love me that much more,"[8] she said.

In order to further her career ambitions, Jennifer decided to audition to become a student at the Fiorello H. LaGuardia High School of Music & Art and Performing Arts, the same school featured in the movie *Fame*. Auditioning for the school was a four-hour process.

Jennifer Aniston (pictured with Chastity Bono, left) attended the Fiorello H. LaGuardia High School of Music & Art and Performing Arts, graduating in 1987.

She had to prepare and perform two monologues and interview with a panel of judges. She was one of over three thousand kids competing for just seventy spots. After a long summer of waiting to hear if she had gotten in, Jennifer got the happy news just days before the school year was to start.

Jennifer loved her new school. "The school was a lot of fun. I couldn't wait to put on my tights and go in there. Any teacher there will tell you that I was the worst. But I didn't care. I didn't get the parts in big plays, but I definitely enjoyed myself,"[9] she said. Jennifer not only enjoyed her classes, she also made a lot of friends, including fellow student Andrea Bendewald. The two girls had a great deal in common, including the fact that their parents were divorced. They became close friends, and their friendship endured to become one of the most important relationships in Jennifer's life.

Jennifer took as many drama classes as she could. Unlike a normal high school, the LaGuardia school focused on the arts, so half of Jennifer's day was spent in drama classes. It was during this

Fame School

Jennifer Aniston attended Fiorello H. LaGuardia High School of Music & Art and Performing Arts. This is the same school that is featured in the 1980 musical *Fame*, which came out a few years before Jennifer was accepted into the school. The movie features high school students from all walks of life bursting into song and dancing on tables during lunch. Although students in real life do not break into spontaneous, perfectly choreographed musical numbers, the movie is accurate in how it portrays the challenging audition process and the ambitions of the students who attend there. In addition to Aniston some of LaGuardia's other famous alumni include Ana Ortiz, Robert De Niro, Al Pacino, Marlon Wayans, and Liza Minnelli. There was also a *Fame* TV show in the 1980s, and a remake of the movie was released in 2009.

time that Jennifer realized that she had a gift for comedic acting. As an adult, Aniston reflected on how this realization came about:

> In performance I had a tendency to be funny instead of going deeper into a scene. In retrospect, I realize that this was something I had been doing most of my life. All through my childhood I had used humor as a survival technique. Whether it was my parents' divorce or trouble with my friends or any of a hundred problems or insecurities that kids go through, I got by through being funny and making people laugh. I think I just did what came naturally to protect myself from hurt.[10]

Jennifer had wanted to be a serious, dramatic actor. In the early 1980s she had attended a Broadway performance of *Children of a Lesser God*. The play is not a comedy; rather, it is the emotional story of a teacher who falls in love with his deaf student. Jennifer was deeply moved by the show, which confirmed her desire to act. "I was sitting in the second or third row, and I was just so blown away, and I walked out saying, 'That's what I want to do,'"[11] she said. Jennifer was so sure she wanted to be a dramatic actor that at first she did not consider her gift for comedy to be much of an asset. However, after she performed a serious scene from Chekhov's *The Three Sisters* only to have her classmates respond with laughter, her teacher, Anthony Abeson, helped her to see why making people laugh is not a bad thing. Abeson recalls: "Afterward, when we went through [the scene], I told her, 'This is a wonderful gift you have.' I really tried to make it clear to her that this was not something to be upset about, that it was really kind of marvelous that she had that ability but that she didn't want to rely upon it to the exclusion of the development of her talent as a whole."[12] Jennifer took his words to heart.

Off to Los Angeles

Jennifer Aniston graduated from high school in 1987. Although her father wanted her to attend college, she decided to pursue her acting career. While still living with her mother, Aniston auditioned for parts during the day and waited tables at night. Aniston's mother supported her acting ambitions, and the two were very close. However, the relationship was often difficult for Aniston, who felt that her mother did not know how to let go. "My mother didn't know where she ended and I began,"[13] said Aniston. In addition, her mother constantly criticized the way she looked, encouraging her to use makeup to make more of her features. "You got to the point where you felt like you were the ugliest duckling on the planet,"[14] said Aniston.

Aniston managed to land roles in a couple of off-Broadway productions. The first was in a one-act community play called *Dancing on Checkers' Grave*, in which Aniston had one of the lead parts. The second was a much bigger production called *For Dear Life*. Although Aniston had only a supporting role and was only onstage for one of the three acts, she enjoyed the experience a great deal. One of her most treasured memories from the production was looking into the audience and seeing the legendary actor Al Pacino. Sitting next to him was actor Diane Keaton. As Aniston delivered one of her funniest lines, Pacino laughed. Aniston was thrilled that she had actually made Al Pacino laugh. However, despite her comedic performance, the play received poor reviews and closed early.

By the time Aniston was twenty years old, her father had moved to Los Angeles. Aniston started staying with him, his wife, and their new baby while auditioning for parts. Soon she moved to Los Angeles for good, taking a low-rent apartment in a communal housing project in the Laurel Canyon area of Los Angeles. Most of the other residents were aspiring actors or writers, and Aniston fit right in. Soon she was part of a fun-loving and close-knit group of friends. The group shared barbecues, parties, girls' nights, and even road trips together. It was during this time that Aniston made another close girlfriend, assistant producer Kristin Hahn. Aniston and Hahn bonded instantly and spent almost every day together for the next few years.

Aniston also had her first real relationship during this time. Although she had dated several boys in high school, her relationship with actor Daniel McDonald was longer and more serious than any of her previous relationships. McDonald also lived in Laurel Canyon and got along well with Aniston's friends.

Jennifer Aniston was cast in the television spin-off of the popular movie Ferris Bueller's Day Off, *but the show was canceled after thirteen episodes.*

Unfortunately, the same could not be said for Aniston's mother, who had moved to Los Angeles to be closer to her children. Dow felt that Aniston's new friends were rude and secretive. Dow's dislike for her daughter's new friends upset Aniston and caused tension in their relationship.

Following Her Dream

To support herself Aniston took a variety of low-paying jobs. In addition to waiting tables, she was a store clerk, a receptionist, a messenger, and a telemarketer. The job she liked the least was telemarketing. She did not like bothering people at home and did not manage to make a single sale. On the acting front Aniston was landing parts, but none that would last.

Aniston's first role was in a 1990 made-for-TV movie called *Camp Cucamonga*. She played a camp counselor, making her one of the older actors in a sea of preteens, who played the campers. Next Aniston landed a role in a pilot for a sitcom called *Molloy*. Molloy was about a teenage girl living with her father and his new family. Aniston played Molloy's older stepsister. Ratings were poor, however, and only seven episodes were made before the show was canceled. Aniston was cast again as an older sister in the TV spin-off of the hugely popular 1986 movie *Ferris Bueller's Day Off*. Unfortunately, audiences did not embrace the TV show with nearly the same enthusiasm as they had the movie, and the show was canceled after thirteen episodes.

Aniston's next role was in a 1993 horror movie called *Leprechaun*, in which she had the female lead. The plot of the movie involves an evil leprechaun who goes on a murderous rampage through a small town, looking for his stolen gold. It did not do well at the box office or with the critics. Film critic Marc Savlov wrote that the actors "end up stockpiling horror movie clichés and invent new and uninteresting methods of bad acting in what is sure to make my ever-expanding list of truly lousy films."[15] Aniston herself was so horrified by the end result that she walked out halfway through the screening.

Although Aniston was getting parts, she lost many more than she got. At one point, when she got a callback that required her to

Jennifer Aniston's first television role was in a made-for-TV movie called Camp Cucamonga, *where she played a camp counselor.*

show up in a leotard, her agent suggested that she lose some weight. Aniston had gained a little by eating her favorites, Big Macs and mayonnaise on white bread, and although she was perhaps a little chunky by Hollywood standards, she was by no means fat. Still, Aniston lost 30 pounds (13.6kg) over the next few months. She had mixed feelings about her weight loss and has even said she was happier before she started dieting. However, she also recognized that the slender actresses were the ones who got the parts. "It's unfortunate that Hollywood puts pressure on women to be thin," said Aniston, "because it sends the wrong message."[16]

Aniston appeared on two episodes of *Herman's Head* and one on *Quantum Leap*, as well as a short-lived comedy sketch show called *The Edge*, before landing a part in yet another sitcom destined for failure. However, for once, hearing her sitcom had failed was good news.

Chapter 2

Friends Like Us

By 1994 twenty-five-year-old Aniston was enjoying her life in Los Angeles. Although none of her projects had lasted, she had earned enough money so that she no longer had to worry about making her rent each month. She had a group of close friends and was once again single, because her boyfriend, Daniel McDonald, had moved to New York to pursue his own career. She spent her free time gardening, hiking, and lunching with friends.

Aniston also had a new sitcom called *Muddling Through*. She played the eldest daughter of a woman who has recently returned home from prison after shooting her cheating husband in the rear end. The family runs a roadside hotel, which Aniston's character kept going during her mother's absence. The pilot received good reviews, and there was reason to think the show might be given a time slot in the fall lineup. However, because Hollywood offers no guarantees, Aniston decided to hedge her bets and audition for another part.

Rachel or Monica?

At first the sitcom about six twenty-something friends living in New York City was to be called *Friends Like Us*. From the start, the show was different from other sitcoms because it was a true ensemble. Rather than having one or two main stars and several supporting cast members, the six stars of *Friends* were equal. Storylines bounced around, sometimes focusing on one character and other times another, but the writers made sure that no one character outshone the others, or at least not for very long.

Like Aniston most of the cast was made up of still-struggling young actors. The one exception was Courteney Cox, who had already amassed a long list of roles on both the small and big screen. Just before landing her role on *Friends*, Cox had starred alongside Jim Carrey in *Ace Ventura: Pet Detective*. She had also appeared in twenty-one episodes of the popular sitcom *Family Ties* with Michael J. Fox.

Aniston had been asked to read for the part of Monica Geller but on reading the script felt that she was more suited for the role of Rachel Green. "She was the part," says executive producer Kevin

Courteney Cox was originally slated to play Rachel Green on Friends, *but she was eventually given the role of Monica Geller, and Jennifer Aniston played Rachel.*

Dancing in the Fountain

At the start of the pilot episode of *Friends*, the six cast members dance in a fountain to the show's theme song, "I'll Be There for You," while the opening credits roll. While subsequent episodes feature other scenes in the opening credits, shots from that first frolic in the fountain have always been included. Although many viewers assumed the scene was filmed in New York's Central Park, it was actually filmed at the Warner Brothers ranch in Burbank, California. Even though the opening credits are less than two minutes long, the scene took hours to shoot, and to make matters worse, it was filmed beginning at 4:00 A.M. on a particularly cold morning. The cast members, who were just getting to know each other, made the best of it, cracking jokes to keep their spirits up.

Seven years later, an episode of *Friends* required that they once again frolic in the fountain. This time the cast made sure that the water was heated and that the shoot did not take more than half an hour.

Bright. "She was funny. She was pretty. It all came through in one big stroke."[17] Coincidentally, Cox was originally slated to play Rachel but felt that she identified more with Monica. The producers wisely listened to their young actors, and each got the part she desired.

The producers of *Friends* knew that Aniston was under contract for *Muddling Through*. Had she not been let out of her contract, Aniston would not have been free to play Rachel in *Friends*. When they were filming the opening shots for *Friends*, the status of *Muddling Through* was still unknown, so Aniston had to sit out of some of the shots in case they needed to replace her later. The producers also knew that they would have to reshoot the first few episodes if Aniston had to be replaced. Fortunately for everyone, soon after *Friends* started shooting, Aniston was released from her contract with *Muddling Through*.

Rachel and Ross

Aniston's first appearance on the pilot episode of *Friends* was when a frantic Rachel surprises everyone by showing up at the Central Perk coffee shop in a wedding dress. Having just left her husband-to-be at the altar, Rachel is looking for Monica, her best friend from high school. Monica introduces her to the other four friends who frequently meet up at Central Perk, and the six are together for the first time.

From the start Rachel is different from the other friends. Unlike the other five, Rachel comes from a privileged background. Living off her father's wealth, she never had to work or even do her own laundry. In the pilot, a newly independent Rachel declares, "I'm going to get one of those . . . job things."[18] Aniston's challenge was to make her character likable and appealing. "In the wrong hands, Rachel is kind of annoying and spoiled and unlikeable. You need an actress who can bring what Jennifer brings to it, for you to really root for this girl,"[19] observed *Friends* cocreator and executive producer David Crane. By the end of the pilot, Rachel has moved in with Monica and gotten her first job as a waitress at Central Perk, where she serves coffee to her new friends.

The romance between Ross and Rachel was one of the most talked-about storylines on **Friends.**

One of the most talked-about storylines of the first few seasons was the romance between Rachel and Ross, played by actor David Schwimmer. For most of the first season, the romance is strictly one-way. Ross is in love with Rachel, but Rachel has no idea that he thinks of her as anything more than a friend. In the beginning no one knew the romance would evolve as it did. Cocreator and executive producer Marta Kauffman explains:

> We didn't realize Ross and Rachel would happen in the beginning. When we first wrote the pilot, it was supposed to be Monica and Joey. But chemistry gives you certain ideas and a TV show does gradually take on a life of its own. It's an interesting process. The characters begin to tell *you* where they're going to go. That's how Ross and Rachel became our central romantic figures.[20]

The Rachel

Friends gained instant popularity, which assured that each of the young actors would have work, at least for a season. Aniston, who had grown accustomed to her shows failing, was pleasantly surprised at the show's success. She said: "I remember when we found out *Friends* was picked up for a whole season. I was baffled by this whole idea that it's going to go on? You mean it doesn't just end after thirteen?"[21]

Not only was the show itself popular, but Aniston's character became an early favorite as well. Although the writers and actors all worked to keep everyone more or less equal, audiences were enthralled with Rachel. As a result, Aniston's face graced the glossy covers and pages of far more magazines than her costars. She was even named one of *People Magazine*'s 25 Most Intriguing People in 1995. The Rachel-Ross romance was most certainly part of the reason for her popularity, as well as her character's bubbly personality, but perhaps the main reason Rachel secured that number one spot was because of her haircut.

Midway through the first season, Aniston had her hair cut by stylist Chris McMillan. The style was a shoulder-length, bouncy shag that framed her face perfectly. Audiences went crazy for the

Jennifer Aniston became so popular during Friends that her hairstyle was dubbed "the Rachel" after her character on the show.

cut that was quickly dubbed "the Rachel." Within days thousands of stylists all across the country were being asked to imitate the cut. About the only person who did not like the new style was Aniston herself. Not only did she hate the cut itself, she also resented having her success attributed to her hair rather than her acting ability.

Falling Out with Mom

As Aniston's fame grew, both her parents seemed to want to spend more time with her. At first Aniston was annoyed with her father, who had not been so attentive before she was famous, but she eventually forgave him.

Things did not go so well with her mother. In February 1996 Nancy Dow gave a TV interview in which she said negative things about her daughter and *Friends*. Soon after, Dow received an angry call from her daughter. Aniston told her mother that she would never forgive her before slamming down the phone. From that

Marcel the Monkey

During the first season of *Friends*, there was a seventh member of the gang—Ross's pet monkey, Marcel. Although the pair of capuchin monkeys that played Marcel were cute, they were not popular on the *Friends* set. Shooting scenes with the monkeys took a great deal of time, and they often behaved badly. One of the monkeys particularly enjoyed pulling Aniston's hair. In addition, their diet of worms

disgusted cast members. It was not long before the writers of the show were looking for ways to write off Marcel. At one point, they considered having Marcel get electrocuted by a toaster, but they opted for a happy ending by having him placed in the San Diego Zoo.

During the first season of Friends, Ross had a pet monkey named Marcel.

point on, Aniston refused to see or talk to her mother. Dow was heartbroken, but she made matters much worse three years later when she published *From Mother and Daughter to Friends: A Memoir*. Contrary to the title, Aniston did not write a single word in the book. The book was instead the story of Dow's own life, in which she reveals a great deal about her daughter's childhood and paints herself as a victim, both in her role as wife and as mother.

Aniston was upset by her own choice to cut off contact from her mother, but she felt it was the right thing to do. "It's a tough one," she says. "That's my irony—my father and I are friends, and my mother and I don't speak. It's a bummer. I miss her. You want to just share it. But I think this is just a necessary break we need to take. Let it heal."[22] Although she could not share her life with her mother, she had plenty of close friends to turn to.

Real Friends

One of the remarkable things about *Friends* is that the six members of the cast really were friends. Aniston's early popularity could have caused rifts in the cast, especially with Courteney Cox, since she originally gave up the role of Rachel. However, this did not happen. "I love the character of Rachel and I think there's no one better to play her than Jennifer," says Cox. "Rachel's character is actually more fun—Monica is uptight. But everything happens for a reason."[23] Rather than becoming rivals, the two became close friends. In the commemorative book *Friends . . . 'til the End*, Cox talks about her friendship with Aniston: "Jennifer is an amazing actress, and I love her so much. She is such a real person and she has so much talent it's unbelievable. Watching her play the dramatic parts on *Friends* and in other roles, and then doing the comedy in such an ethereal way, it's just fantastic. She's like my sister. I adore that girl. She's my friend for life."[24]

Cox and Aniston's friendship was just a part of the unique bond that all six of the cast members shared. "We all bonded instantly,"[25] said Aniston. From the start the producers encouraged the group to do things together because they felt that if the actors had chemistry off the set, it would transfer to their on-screen performances. They went to group dinners, viewings of the show, and even a trip to Las Vegas. The six cast members became close friends, joking together on the set, supporting and encouraging each other, and always ready with a hug or a backrub. Aniston, who has always been happiest when surrounded by friends, thrived in this environment. In *Friends . . . 'til the End*, she said:

> Every single person in this cast is my family. They feel like a part of my family. And what I appreciate about them is how everybody's work is consistent and everybody's work is committed. What I admire is the evolution of everybody's craft, which has been so much fun to watch unfold as we all learned our comedy chops. We've all learned together how to be better actors. I learn from these guys every single day I walk on the set.[26]

Even in contract negotiations the cast stuck together. During the first season the actors each got the same salary: $22,500 per episode.

The friendship between Jennifer Aniston and Courteney Cox was real both on and off the show. All six Friends cast members had a tight bond and supported each other during the show's ten seasons.

For the second season, each cast member negotiated independently for his or her salary, with the result that some of the cast were paid more than others. For the third season, led by David Schwimmer, the cast decided to negotiate as a collective rather than individually, a decision that did not please the studio. This meant pay cuts for both Aniston and Schwimmer. However, it put the six friends in a very powerful position, since there could be no show without all of them. "There's none of this thing of . . . 'Well if one or two of you leave we can go on without you,'" says Aniston. "No way is it that. We all do it—or nobody does it."[27] The strategy paid off because it kept all the cast members together for the whole ten-season run of the show, and their salaries continued to rise until each was making a million dollars per episode for the final two seasons.

*Friends*mania

One of the many reasons the cast members bonded so closely was that they shared the road to fame together. "We were sort of side-swiped when the show exploded," says Aniston. "We were not paying attention to out *there*, we were just focused on in *here*. We were thinking, 'If we're having this much fun, hopefully, it's translating.'"[28]

It was translating in a big way. People loved the show. During that first year, the show's theme song, "I'll Be There for You" by the Rembrandts, was played regularly on radio stations across the country. Coffee shops decorated not unlike Central Perk began popping up everywhere. Cast members could not appear in public without being asked for autographs by eager fans. There were *Friends* posters, calendars, and Web sites. Magazine publishers begged them to appear on their covers. It was Aniston who first realized that they were doing too much in the way of publicity. Costar Lisa Kudrow recalls:

> That's where I give Jennifer credit, because hers was the voice I remember most clearly when Warner Bros. asked us to do the Diet Coke commercials. She said, 'It's too much. We're doing *too* many covers, and it's *too* much.' And we could have listened to her. But we didn't. Still, I remember Jennifer was very aware of too much publicity. We're

on the cover of everything and people are getting sick of seeing us and she turned out to be right.[29]

The Diet Coke commercials were the final straw in what turned out to be too much exposure. In what has been called "*Friends* backlash," the press suddenly went sour on the show and the cast during the second season. "We were just doing a job and loving it. It had great success, and we were thrilled. Then it got bigger and bigger, and then, out of nowhere, one day you're reading that people are really annoyed,"[30] said Aniston. The criticism was hard on the entire cast, and the six turned to each other for support. Fortunately, the backlash did not stick, and the show maintained its popularity.

Awards and Honors

In its first season *Friends* ranked number eight in the ratings, which means it was the eighth most popular show that year. The numbers just got better from there. It was in the top five every season after that, taking the number one slot in season eight. The

Valentine Surprises

Jennifer Aniston has a knack for picking romantic men. Two times while shooting *Friends*, she came back to her dressing room to find a special valentine surprise. The first was in 1997 when she was dating Tate Donovan. Donovan got Aniston an Australian shepherd puppy, wrapped a big red bow around his neck, and put him on her chair so that she would see him as soon as she walked in. Aniston loved the puppy, which she named Enzo, and thought it was the most romantic thing anyone had ever done for her.

Four years later, on Valentine's Day 2001, Aniston found fifteen hundred red and pink roses in her dressing room. On the mirror, spelled out in red rose petals, were the words "I love my wife." Aniston was touched by the romantic gesture from her husband, Brad Pitt.

The cast of Friends *was doing so much publicity that a "Friends backlash" occurred during the show's second season. It did not stick, and the show remained hugely popular.*

show was not just popular with TV audiences, it was also a hit with the critics. Although it garnered a few harsh words during the first season, reviews got progressively better. It was not long before the show was being favorably compared with iconic sitcoms such as *M*A*S*H*, *Cheers*, and *Seinfeld*.

The show was popular at awards time as well. Over its ten-year run, the show was nominated for sixty-three Emmy awards and won six of them. In 2002 the show received an award in the Outstanding Comedy Series category. That same year, Aniston won for Outstanding Lead Actress in a Comedy Series. During her speech she praised the cast and writers, saying: "This has been the greatest nine years of my entire life. To work with this cast who make me better, every day, who inspire me every day. Our writers, the most brilliant writers in television and I would not be here, any of us would not be here without you guys."[31]

The show won the People's Choice award six times; once for Favorite New Comedy Series and five times for Favorite Comedy Series. The show, as well as Aniston, was popular with teens, too. *Friends* won six Teen Choice Awards for Best Comedy, while Aniston

In 2002 Jennifer Aniston won the Emmy award for
Outstanding Lead Actress in a Comedy Series for Friends.
In her speech, she praised the cast and crew.

won three for Best Actress in a Comedy. The show did not do well with the Golden Globes; however, Aniston did win one in 2003, the only *Friends* actor to do so.

Trying for the Big Screen

As television actors become popular, they frequently get offered movie scripts. As a result, a popular TV series will sometimes lose its biggest stars to the big screen. The producers of *Friends* did not want to lose any of their cast, so they worked hard to accommodate their actors' schedules. It was often challenging to film when one of the actors was off doing a movie, but the strategy was a good one; the actors got their chances at the box office, and no one left the show.

Although her new fame on *Friends* brought plenty of scripts her way, Aniston started small with supporting roles. Her first movie after achieving fame, *Dream for an Insomniac*, was from a small studio and was not widely released. In her next movie, the 1996 romantic comedy *She's the One*, Aniston played the whiny and irritating wife of one of the two brothers that take center stage. She also had a small part as a best friend in the romantic comedy *'Til There Was You* in 1997. While these movies were not terrible, they were not terribly good either, and the general opinion was that Aniston was playing it safe by taking roles that were not particularly interesting or challenging.

Aniston took her first starring role in the 1997 romantic comedy *Picture Perfect*. In this movie Aniston played Kate, an aspiring advertising executive who is told that her freewheeling, single lifestyle is holding her back careerwise. The company she works for would prefer she was more stable and married. Kate solves this problem by finding a man to pretend to be her fiancé. Although she takes center stage in this movie, again the role is not that challenging, and the movie, though amusing, is nothing special. In her review for the *San Francisco Chronicle*, film critic Ruthe Stein wrote, "'Picture Perfect,' yet another romantic comedy about a career woman who has everything except a man, is Jennifer Aniston's attempt to break out of her TV role. But she doesn't have the magic on the big screen to make us forget where she came from."[32]

Jennifer Aniston's first starring role in a film was in the romantic comedy **Picture Perfect** *in 1997.*

Aniston's next movie, *The Object of My Affection*, did not do much better. In this romantic comedy Aniston plays a woman who gets pregnant by one man but chooses to raise the baby with another, who happens to be gay. The movie, though amusing, was mired in an overcrowded storyline. Once again, Aniston had made a movie-length sitcom. While none of her movies had completely failed, her next film, *The Thin Pink Line*, did. Although it was loaded with stars, including *Friends* costar David Schwimmer, Mike Myers, and Will Ferrell, the movie went straight to video.

Even though her early movies did not do well at the box office, working on movie sets was a good experience for Aniston. She learned a great deal about making movies and established herself as a dedicated actor who could not only do comedy, but drama as well. *Picture Perfect* director Glen Gordon Caron said of Aniston: "Very few people can be funny and intelligent. She's got the chops to be a wonderful dramatic actress."[33]

Chapter 3

Hollywood's Golden Couple

After the first season of *Friends*, Aniston bought a two-bedroom house in the Hollywood Hills. Although not large by superstar standards, the house had a pool, a stunning view of the ocean, and trees that kept her out of range of curious fans and aggressive photographers. She decorated with antiques that she found herself on weekend afternoons and put in a Jacuzzi and a gym. Talking about her yard, Aniston said: "It's teeny, teeny, tiny, but it's my favorite place in the world, up here. When the sun is setting, I have five little bunny rabbits that sit out on the lawn, and there are quail and hummingbirds. It's a really special spot."[34]

A frequent and welcome visitor to Aniston's home was her boyfriend, actor Tate Donovan. The two met in November 1995, while Aniston was filming the second season of *Friends*. At the time, Donovan was starring in a sitcom called *Partners*, which was canceled after just twenty-two episodes. Aniston and Donovan dated for two and half years and were very much in love. "He's so real, so honest, so funny, so kind and considerate. He's all these things meshed into one perfect guy,"[35] said Aniston. Although they did exchange commitment rings, despite rumors to the contrary, the two were never engaged. Even though the relationship seemed promising, as time passed things grew stressful. Aniston became an even bigger star, while Donovan's career faltered. Rumors spread that Donovan was intimidated by Aniston's success. In addition, Aniston wanted to have children someday, and Donovan did not. The two grew apart and eventually broke up in early 1998.

A Bigger Star

Soon after her breakup with Donovan, Aniston went on a blind date with actor Brad Pitt, a man who, unlike her last boyfriend, had no reason to feel intimidated by her success. The date was set up by their agents, but it was not truly "blind," since Aniston and Pitt were both household names. By the time he met Aniston, thirty-four-year-old Pitt had a long list of movie credits, including *A River Runs Through It*, *Legends of the Fall*, and *Seven Years in Tibet*. In addition, in 1995 he had been named *People* magazine's Sexiest Man Alive. Pitt was considered one of the most desirable men in show business. Like Aniston, Pitt had also recently suffered a breakup—he had been engaged to actor Gwyneth Paltrow.

Although they were frequently seen together in cozy restaurants and on romantic getaways, for months Aniston and Pitt refused to admit that they were romantically involved. They attended events such as award shows and the opening of Pitt's 1998 movie *Meet Joe Black* in separate limousines and did not sit together, something that frustrated both fans and photographers. "A picture of them together doesn't take away from his movie or his stardom. It's better just to pose together and look happy. Everybody knows they're going together. They should stop this baloney. It's very immature for them to play mind games like that,"[36] said *New York Daily News* photographer Richard Corkery.

Aniston, however, had a very different view of why they were keeping their relationship private. When asked about Pitt, Aniston told *Rolling Stone* reporter Nancy Collins, "I can't talk about it. I'm sorry. I'm not withholding, just preserving something that's mine." After being prodded further, she added: "My responsibility to the public is my work—not what goes on in my private life. To talk about a relationship trivializes something that's nobody's business. . . . I'll just tell you that this is the happiest time of my life—that I'm happier than I've ever been. I'm not saying why, it's for a lot of reasons: work, love, family, just life—all of it."[37]

Aniston turned thirty soon after that interview. To celebrate Aniston's birthday as well as Valentine's Day, which was three days later, Pitt chartered a plane to Acapulco, Mexico. They brought along nine of their closest friends and spent the weekend partying

Jennifer Aniston met Brad Pitt on a blind date. For months after they began dating they refused to admit that they were romantically involved.

at a private, forty-nine-room villa on the beach. Pitt had hired three cooks to make sure there was always plenty to eat and drink. The group played in the surf, danced until dawn, and watched fireworks over the Pacific that had been set off for Valentine's Day.

Back at home Pitt often came to visit Aniston on the set of *Friends*, where he enjoyed joking around with the other cast members. When filming was finished for the season, the two took a trip to Spain, coming back in time to attend Courteney Cox's wedding to David Arquette on June 12. Aniston and Pitt finally appeared together as a couple the following September at the 1999 Emmy Awards. Arm in arm, the two happily posed for pictures on the red carpet. In an October interview with *Rolling Stone*, Pitt admitted to being in love with Aniston and explained some of what he found appealing about her: "She's fantastic, she's complicated, she's wise, she's fair, she has great empathy for others . . . and she's just so cool."[38]

Just a few months later, Aniston and Pitt hopped onstage with pop singer Sting at his concert at the Beacon Theater in Manhattan. Aniston joined Sting at the microphone to sing "Fill 'Er Up." During the song Pitt put his arm around Aniston, grabbed her left hand, and showed Sting and the audience the diamond ring that now graced her finger. Although publicity spokespeople for both Aniston and Pitt denied it, the couple was clearly engaged. They had actually gotten engaged after only five months of dating, but they did not tell anyone. "That was so fun, just to have that be our own secret,"[39] said Aniston.

A Fairytale Wedding

Jennifer Aniston and Brad Pitt were married on the evening of July 29, 2000. The wedding, which was estimated to have cost a million dollars, was a top-secret affair. The location was a secret, even to the two hundred invited guests, in order to make sure that the paparazzi would not ruin their special day. The guests included most of the cast of *Friends* (Matt LeBlanc was on location for a movie outside the country and so could not attend), as well as actors Cameron Diaz, Salma Hayek, and Edward Norton. The guests gathered at the Malibu High School parking lot, where they took shuttles to the luxurious Malibu es-

Brad's Past Loves

Brad Pitt dated several actresses before he met Jennifer Aniston. One of his first relationships, with Robin Givens, lasted just six months in the late 1980s. In 1990, while still a struggling actor, Pitt met sixteen-year-old Juliette Lewis while they were making a movie together. Despite the fact that Pitt was nine years older than Lewis, the two fell in love and moved in together. They broke up three years later as Pitt was gaining popularity. Pitt's next relationship was with Gwyneth Paltrow. The pair met while filming *Seven*, moved in together, and even got engaged. They seemed to be blissfully in love, and Pitt was eager to get married, but in June 1997, just six months after announcing their engagement, the couple broke up. At least in

public, Pitt did not appear to be grieving the lost relationship. Paltrow, on the other hand, said Pitt had broken her heart and it would never be the same again. Less than a year after his breakup with Paltrow, Pitt met Aniston.

Before Jennifer, Brad Pitt dated Gwyneth Paltrow. The couple broke up six months after announcing their engagement.

tate owned by TV producer Marcy Carsey that the couple had rented for the evening.

The estate, which overlooked the ocean, was decorated with fifty thousand flowers as well as candles made from brown sugar and flown in from Thailand. Lotus flowers floated in a fountain that had been made especially for the occasion. A string quartet was hired to entertain the guests while they waited for the ceremony to begin.

Music for the ceremony was provided by a six-piece band and a forty-member gospel choir. The choir sang "Love Is the Greatest Thing" while Aniston was escorted down the aisle by her father. She wore a fifty-two-thousand-dollar silk and satin designer gown and a veiled crystal and pearl crown. Her bridesmaids, best

Brad Pitt and Jennifer Aniston were married in a top-secret ceremony on July 29, 2000.

It Is a Ring Thing

The ring that Brad Pitt gave Jennifer Aniston was no ordinary engagement ring. Pitt took seven months to codesign it with renowned Italian jeweler Silvia Damiani. The design, which is meant to symbolize eternity, features a pair of diamond-studded platinum spirals surrounding a larger central diamond. Pitt and Aniston were so pleased with the ring that they went back to the Damiani company to design their wedding bands.

However, trouble arose when Damiani began selling copies of the bands to the public, breaching the agreement it had made with Aniston and Pitt not to replicate the rings. The couple filed a $50 million lawsuit against Damiani, demanding that sales be stopped immediately. The case never made it to court. Instead, Damiani forged an alliance with the couple in which Pitt agreed to design a line of jewelry for the company and Aniston agreed to appear in advertisements to promote it.

friend from high school Andrea Bendewald and best friend from her early days in Los Angeles, Kristin Hahn, wore pale green silk.

During the ceremony, the two exchanged vows they had written themselves. Among other things, Pitt promised to "split the difference on the thermostat,"[40] and Aniston promised always to make his "favorite banana milkshake." They also exchanged more traditional vows. They had planned to say them together, but unlike the professional actor that she is, Aniston missed her cue, exclaiming, "Oh, I've never done this before!"[41]

At the reception there was yet another band, dancing, plenty of gourmet food, including a six-tiered wedding cake, and after the sun set, a thirteen-minute fireworks show. "It was a beautiful wedding,"[42] said Aniston's father.

One person who was not there to comment was Aniston's mother. Aniston was still not talking to her mother after she had written her tell-all book. "I can't believe I got married and my mother has never met the person I married," she said tearfully to *Vanity Fair* reporter Leslie Bennetts. "I never would have believed it, when I was 17, if you had told me that would happen."[43]

The Happy Couple

The newly married couple lived in Aniston's relatively modest two-bedroom home for the first few years of their marriage. In public they were loving and affectionate toward each other. At home they enjoyed spending time together, often doing everyday things like walking the dogs or watching movies. "It's funny, people have this idea of a life that's so glamorous, but it couldn't be more boring and normal—sitting at home, ordering take-out. It's fun to be home. I'm such a nester, and we're ridiculous homebodies,"[44] said Aniston.

The couple also enjoyed socializing. They frequently hosted friends for drinks, dinners, and game nights. Some of these friends were people Aniston had been close to for many years, like Bendewald and Hahn. Others were newer friends, like singer Melissa Etheridge and actor Catherine Keener. The couple also enjoyed spending time with *Friends* costar Courteney Cox and her husband, David.

Although they valued their time together, they were often apart, pursuing their individual careers. Both Pitt and Aniston "have a drive for success," says Etheridge, "but it never overshadows their drive for a healthy, happy life. They enjoy their careers, but if it was ever bad for them, they would so drop it."[45] Pitt had made *Fight Club* while they were courting and worked on several projects early in the first decade of the 2000s, including *The Mexican*, *Spy Game*, and *Ocean's Eleven*. However, even when filming, Pitt frequently flew home to see Aniston, even if they could only spend twenty-four hours together.

Brad on *Friends*

In 2001 Pitt took a break from the big screen to appear with his wife in an episode of *Friends*. Often called the "Golden Couple," Pitt and Aniston were easily the most popular couple in Hollywood. Both friends and fans considered them to be a model of marital bliss. The *Friends* writers took advantage of the couple's obvious adoration for each other by creating a character for Pitt that was his exact opposite.

In the Thanksgiving episode, Pitt played Will, an unpopular and previously overweight classmate from Rachel's high school. During the episode it comes out that Will, along with Ross, was a cofounder of the "We Hate Rachel Club" back in high school and furthermore that he and Ross started a vicious rumor about Rachel. Rachel of course, has no memory of treating Will unkindly and is confused by his hostility toward her.

Brad Pitt appeared on an episode of Friends *with his wife in 2001. He played Will, who went to high school with Rachel and started a "We Hate Rachel Club" with Ross.*

Pitt worked well with the regular cast members, all of whom he knew well from his frequent visits to Aniston on the set. Pitt shared Aniston's dressing room through the four days of rehearsing for the show. Aniston wanted her husband to enjoy his experience on *Friends* and to be successful. "It was terribly important to her that he have a good time and feel really good about doing it," said *Friends* executive producer David Crane. "It was really sweet to see just how much she was looking out for him."[46]

The Good Girl

Like Pitt, Aniston also made several movies while the two were dating. In the successful 1999 comedy *Office Space*, she once again played a supporting role, this time as a waitress and the love interest of a discontented office worker. Although Aniston did not get much screen time, she did well with what she had. *San Francisco Examiner* movie critic Craig Marine said, "She plays the role just right, not trying to act like a big star, and even if she gets a bit lost in this movie, it bodes well for her movie career—not that she needs any help."[47] Although the movie had only a mediocre showing at the box office, it has since become a cult classic that will not likely be forgotten anytime soon.

After doing the voice for a character in the animated movie *The Iron Giant*, Aniston played another supporting part in the poorly received 2001 movie *Rock Star*. In 2002 Aniston took on a different kind of role in the independent dark comedy *The Good Girl*. Aniston was immediately drawn to the project when she saw the script. "I pretty much fell in love with it by page five,"[48] she said. To prepare for the part, Aniston worked with a dialect coach to perfect a tired Southern twang. Her character, Justine, is a frustrated thirty-year-old cashier who is stuck in a small Texas town with a job she hates and a husband she no longer loves. The reason this film was such a success for Aniston is that she finally broke away from the funny, bouncy sitcom character she was known for. In contrast, Justine is drab, worn down, and defeated. "At no point in time during the film was I reminded of the airheaded, schmaltzy Rachel whom she portrays in the ever-popular *Friends*," wrote film critic Mark Sells. "In fact, this is a landmark

Aniston received big screen kudos for her portrayal of Justine in the independent dark comedy **The Good Girl.**

film for Aniston, who successfully sheds her stereotyped persona of sitcom to earn big screen kudos."[49]

A Place to Call Home

In June 2001 Aniston acquired a big house to match her "big screen kudos." Pitt and Aniston bought a 10,000-square-foot (929 sq. m) Beverly Hills mansion for $13.5 million. However, they did not move in to the house right away. Instead, they planned an extensive renovation project. Originally, they had hoped to move in by March 2002, but that date came and went and the house was not nearly done. In the end, they did not move in until July 2003.

The renovated mansion boasted a tennis court, pool and spa, a game room, an English-style pub, and a professional screening room. The house also had a nursery, which, like most of the rest of the house, was designed by Pitt. The couple was clearly thinking about starting a family. "I always thought two or three children, but Brad's definitely seven," said Aniston in 2001. "He loves the idea of having a huge family. But you just never know. Whatever will be, will be."[50] A year later she seemed even more ready for children. In 2002 while filming the ninth season of *Friends*, which both cast and crew thought would be the last, she told *Entertainment Weekly*, "In my mind I'm done. I want to start my family."[51]

Birthday Bash

Jennifer Aniston thought she was going for a quiet dinner with her husband to celebrate her thirty-third birthday. However, when they arrived at the Japanese restaurant Katana, Aniston was thrilled to find a surprise party waiting for her. Pitt had invited Aniston's closest friends and had gotten the baker to make a miniature replica of their wedding cake. Pitt even gave a special toast in honor of his wife, saying: "Happy birthday Jen. You're my best friend, my soulmate and the one I'll spend eternity with. I don't know what I did to deserve you. But I thank God every day that you came into my life. I love you, now and forever." For her gift, Pitt gave Aniston a platinum bracelet with two charms. One of the charms was an antique, diamond-encrusted locket that encased a picture of the couple on one of their first dates. The other charm was engraved with her birthday and the words "I love you Brad."

Quoted in Internet Movie Database, "Brad's $21,000 Bash for Jennifer," February 14, 2002. www.imdb.com/name/nm0000098/news?year=2002;start=41.

Box Office Hits with Bruce and Polly

Aniston may have wanted to take a break to start a family, but in reality she was busier than ever. While filming the ninth season of *Friends*, Aniston made two movies that were both destined to take the number one slot at the box office: *Bruce Almighty*, which was released in 2003, and *Along Came Polly*, which came out the following year. In both movies she played the girlfriend to a popular male lead; however, the two girlfriends had completely different personalities. In *Bruce Almighty* she played opposite comedic actor Jim Carrey. Carrey was a much bigger star, commanding a $25 million salary for the film, while Aniston made $5 million. Carrey was in his element playing a self-centered, dissatisfied TV news reporter who is given godlike powers. The movie was clearly focused on Carrey and his outrageous antics. That left Aniston, who played a mild-mannered kindergarten teacher, mostly just to react to whatever bizarre things Carrey did. Movie critic Andrew O'Hehir notes, "Aniston, although likable as always, is squandered on a nothing role here."[52]

In *Along Came Polly* Aniston found herself once again contrasting her role to the lead actor, Ben Stiller. Stiller played a kindhearted but overly cautious insurance assessor, and Aniston took on the role of Polly Prince, his freewheeling, commitment-phobic girlfriend. Although the movie is a lighthearted comedy, filming it was not without its challenges. Aniston had to work with a ferret, which bit Stiller and which Aniston called a "big rat." Aniston also had to learn to salsa dance. She explains in an interview with IGN why that was difficult:

> I took two [classes]. I was supposed to take more, but I didn't. It was good. Thank god we got that. We had two days in New York shooting and then the next bit for me was all of the salsa dancing. And it was five days straight. My feet looked like raw meat. It was just disgusting. I don't know how those dancers do it. But it was so much fun. And then right after we shot those six days I broke my toe. So thank god we took care of all of that stuff. So I limped through the rest of the movie.[53]

Jennifer Aniston starred in Along Came Polly with Ben Stiller in 2004.

Although Aniston looked great on the dance floor, most of the laughs came from Stiller's attempts to escape his overly cautious tendencies. Movie critic David Edelstein notes: "Aniston is surprisingly good here—throaty and soft and slightly detached. She resists the impulse to go zany and hits a couple of authentically weird (inward) notes, but the character never really comes into focus—not even fleeting screwball focus."[54]

With two blockbuster films under her belt and yet another successful year of *Friends*, Aniston had achieved superstar status. Confirming her rise to the top, *Forbes* magazine ranked her number one on its list of the 100 Top Celebrities in 2003. Based on wealth and fame, the magazine noted that Aniston had been on the covers of thirteen magazines in the past twelve months, more than any other celebrity, and that she had brought in a whopping $35 million in pay. With her multimillion-dollar mansion and her superstar husband, Aniston's life seemed to be perfect.

Chapter 4

Time for Good-Byes

In January 2003 Jennifer Aniston won the Golden Globe for Best Actress in a Comedy Series for *Friends*. In her acceptance speech Aniston excitedly thanked her costars, the studio, and the writers but forgot to thank, or even mention, her husband, Brad. Although she realized her mistake during the backstage interview and corrected it by thanking him then, people began to wonder if something was amiss in what had always appeared to be an ideal marriage.

Rumors were fueled by the fact that Pitt was often away, filming movies on location. The couple had recently founded a film production company called Plan B. In 2003 Pitt was filming Plan B's first movie, *Troy*. The epic movie, which was destined for failure, required five months of filming in Malta, an island off the coast of Italy. However, the rumors did not get serious until Pitt started filming the action-packed romantic comedy *Mr. and Mrs. Smith* with actor Angelina Jolie.

Mrs. Smith

Twice divorced, Jolie was known for her intense love relationships, smoldering sexuality, and somewhat wild, outspoken personality. By the time she met Pitt, Jolie was deeply involved with the United Nations High Commissioner for Refugees, often traveling to remote and even dangerous locations with refugee volunteers. She was also a new mother, having adopted Cambodian orphan Maddox in 2002. Aniston and Jolie met once briefly, before filming started on *Mr. and Mrs. Smith*. Aniston introduced herself to Jolie and said: "Brad is so excited about working with you. I hope you guys have a really good time."[55]

Pitt and Jolie hit it off from the start. They worked extremely well together, a fact that was clear to everyone, from the other cast members to the critics who reviewed the movie. "Their onscreen chemistry is 100 percent them," noted director Doug Liman, who added that "the sparks were evident from the first day of shooting."[56] Tabloid writers jumped on the pair's obvious chemistry, speculating that their mutual attraction was not just for the cameras. Paparazzi followed them everywhere, hoping to get a picture that would prove the two were romantically involved. However, although they were

Brad Pitt and Angelina Jolie starred in Mr. and Mrs. Smith. *Director Doug Liman noticed the sparks between the costars from the start.*

sometimes seen together in public, they never did anything to indicate they were anything more than good friends.

Aniston, too, denied anything was going on between her husband and Jolie. When asked about the alleged affair, Aniston replied: "We try to laugh, of course. You protect each other. But it's Hollywood, baby. It's like every day, every week, something new."[57] Although Aniston and Pitt were not seeing much of each other at the time, they seemed to enjoy the time they did have and were very affectionate toward one another whenever they appeared in public. They even talked publicly about their plans to start a family.

However, privately, things may not have been as they appeared. Aniston later told *Vanity Fair* reporter Leslie Bennetts that Pitt had become distant and emotionally unavailable soon after filming on *Mr. and Mrs. Smith* began. Aniston was filming the final episodes of *Friends*, and she needed her husband's support. "He just wasn't there for me,"[58] Aniston said. Pitt did not even show up for the taping of the final episode, though he claimed it was because he did not want to know how the show ended until it was broadcast later that year.

Friends . . . 'til the End

The tenth season of *Friends* was a bit of a surprise for everyone involved. Everyone was sure that the ninth season would be the last; however, near the end the cast agreed to come back and do one more season. One of the conditions for the new contract was

After the airing of the last episode of Friends, the cast appeared on "The Tonight Show with Jay Leno." Pictured from left are Matthew Perry, Lisa Kudrow, Jennifer Aniston, Courteney Cox, host Jay Leno, Matt LeBlanc, and David Schwimmer. The final season of Friends was very emotional for all six cast members.

that the season be cut to just eighteen episodes rather than the usual twenty-four. Although she eventually agreed to do another season, Aniston resisted the idea at first. Not only was she eager to start a family, she also had reservations about the show itself. Aniston explained during an interview on NBC's *Dateline* the day before the last episode aired: "I had a couple issues that I was dealing with. I wanted it to end where people still loved us and we were on a high. And I was also feeling like how much more of Rachel is in me. How many more stories are there to tell for all of us before [we're] just pathetic. . . . And now of course, I'm just terrified and I don't want it to end at all."[59]

The final season was emotional for the entire cast, but despite her original misgivings about a tenth season, of all the cast members Aniston seemed to have the most difficult time with the ending of the show. "I think Jennifer probably won't be able to breathe. I think she started crying the first day we got here this year,"[60] commented close friend and costar Courteney Cox. "I didn't think that it would feel this heart-wrenching and sad,"[61] said Aniston.

Clocking in at 236 episodes, the final *Friends* was taped on January 23, 2004, in front of an audience of 250 friends and family. Tears flowed freely during the taping, and several cast members had to have their makeup redone before the show even started. Gifts were exchanged, and cast members took turns signing yearbooks that had been specially made for them by the producers.

The central storyline for the two-part finale focuses on the on-again, off-again relationship between Ross and Rachel. After a dramatic but disappointing airport scene, Ross and Rachel reunite for good, finally giving millions of fans the ending they had spent ten years hoping for. The much-anticipated finale was broadcast on May 6, 2004, to an audience of over 50 million viewers. Fans seemed happy with the ending, and although there were some negative reviews, many critics thought it was a fitting conclusion. *USA Today* critic Robert Bianco wrote: "It may have been impossible for any one episode to live up to the hype and expectations built up around the *Friends* finale, but this hour probably came as close as fans could have reasonably hoped. . . . Ultimately, the two-hour package did exactly what it was supposed to do. It wrapped up the story while reminding us why we liked the show and will miss it."[62]

Rumor Has It

By the time the finale aired in early May 2004, rumors of an affair between Pitt and Jolie were rampant. Publicly, all parties continued to deny that any such affair existed. On May 10 Pitt and Aniston attended the premier of *Troy* together and were openly affectionate. Later that month Pitt took a break from filming *Mr. and Mrs. Smith* to work on *Ocean's Twelve* in Italy. Aniston joined him there, where again the couple was affectionate and seemed to be happy. Although some refused to believe the rumors, others speculated that their public displays of affection were nothing more than an act.

By August Pitt was finishing *Mr. and Mrs. Smith* with Jolie, and Aniston had started filming *Rumor Has It*, a confusing comedy loosely associated with the 1967 classic Dustin Hoffman movie, *The Graduate*. Unlike *The Graduate*, *Rumor Has It* was not a huge hit and got mixed reviews. Many critics felt that Aniston's performance was lacking. *New York Sun* critic Meghan Keane was particularly harsh, saying that it was a mistake to put such a large film on Aniston's shoulders and calling her "the biggest obstacle to the film's success."[63] In contrast, William Arnold of the *Seattle Post Intelligencer* thought she did well, writing: "Aniston is thoroughly appealing. Her inner turmoil is palpable, she's endearing without seeming to be trying too hard at it."[64]

As it turned out, Arnold's comment about Aniston's "inner turmoil" was more accurate than he probably imagined. In a 2006 interview with *Vogue*, when asked about *Rumor Has It*, Aniston was clear about her feelings about the movie as well as her emotional state during the filming. "The worst experience of my life. The worst experience, the worst film," she said. "And for me, personally, I was going through a horrible time. I wasn't at my best as an actor. I was unmotivated by it."[65]

Next Aniston filmed the thriller *Derailed* with English actor Clive Owen. The movie was violent and contained rape and murder scenes, representing a sharp departure from her usual romantic comedy. Aniston decided to do the film not only because she felt it would challenge her, but also because veteran actor Julia Roberts had told her that if she had the chance to work with

Godmother Jen

Jennifer Aniston is godmother to Courteney Cox and David Arquette's daughter, Coco.

Although 2005 was a tough year for Jennifer Aniston, there was at least one bright spot. On April 9 Aniston became godmother to Courteney Cox and David Arquette's ten-month-old daughter, Coco. The service was held at the Birmingham, Alabama, church where Cox had attended services as a child. During the baptismal service, Aniston held Coco and agreed to provide moral guidance for her. Cox was confident that Aniston would be a wonderful godmother, and Aniston has lived up to her friend's expectations. According to Cox, Aniston spends time with Coco nearly every weekend. Coco adores Aniston and calls her "Noona," the Greek word for godmother.

Owen, she should take it. The two worked well together, and Aniston clearly impressed Owen, who said:

No one has seen her do this kind of part before, and it was a very smart choice to book Jennifer in. The bottom line is, she's a really classy actress—incredibly smart and sensitive. [She is] just hugely refreshing, completely unstarry, completely uncomplicated. There was no fuss. With big stars you never know quite what to expect. But for somebody who's lived under the spotlight for so long, she's incredibly sorted out and grounded. That was inspiring—that you can be a real human being. It takes an enormous amount of intelligence to keep rooted amidst that glare.[66]

Aniston was dealing with personal turmoil during the filming of Rumor Has It.

The film did poorly both with critics and at the box office. However, Aniston was not nearly as upset with *Derailed* as she was with *Rumor Has It*, saying: "*Derailed* didn't shine. It kind of . . . derailed. Thrillers are tough. I'm glad I did it, but I don't need to do those kinds of movies. It's kind of like caviar. I don't need to have it again."[67]

Good-Bye to Brad

Aniston had spent most of 2004 hiding her feelings, pretending, along with Pitt, that everything was fine in public, while in private their marriage was falling apart. On January 7, 2005, Aniston and Pitt stopped pretending and issued a joint statement proclaiming their separation:

> We would like to announce that after seven years together we have decided to formally separate. For those who follow these sorts of things, we would like to explain that our separation is not the result of any of the speculation reported by the tabloid media. This decision is the result of much thoughtful consideration. We happily remain committed and caring friends with great love and admiration for one another. We ask in advance for your kindness and sensitivity in the coming months.[68]

Aniston's friends and fans, and reportedly even Pitt's mother, hoped the couple would reconcile, but it was not to be. On March 25, 2005, less than three months after the couple separated, Aniston filed for divorce, citing irreconcilable differences as the reason for the split. The proceedings went smoothly, and Aniston and Pitt were officially divorced on October 2, 2005.

What Happened to the Golden Couple?

From the moment that Pitt and Aniston announced their separation, the media speculated on what went wrong for what had seemed to be the perfect couple. Despite denials by all the parties involved, the alleged Pitt-Jolie affair was at the top of the list. Speculation reached a fevered pitch in late April 2005, when *US Weekly* published pictures of Pitt, Jolie, and Jolie's son, Maddox, frolicking on the beach at a romantic resort in Africa. "The world was shocked, and I was shocked,"[69] said Aniston. A few months later Aniston was shocked again by a sixty-page photo spread of Pitt and Jolie in *W* magazine. The spread, called *Domestic Bliss*, was conceptualized by Pitt and featured 1960s style photos of Pitt, Jolie, and five adorable little boys. Many of the shots were family scenes, such as everyone at the dinner table or the children playing in a wading pool with the parents nearby. Aniston was hurt by the photos, commenting, "There's a sensitivity chip that's missing."[70]

Brad Pitt and Angelina Jolie arrive at Narita Airport in Japan with Maddox and Zahara to promote **Mr. and Mrs. Smith.** *The media speculated about what went wrong with the Pitt-Aniston marriage, and the alleged Pitt-Jolie affair was at the top of everyone's list.*

The pictures of Pitt with children, first Jolie's son and then the *W* photo spread, reinforced another theory about why Pitt and Aniston had split up: Pitt clearly wanted to be a father, but the media was not so sure about Aniston's desire for parenthood. Tabloids claimed that Aniston had put her career first and refused to start a family. Aniston responded to these accusations with anger, saying: "I've never in my life said I didn't want to have children. I did and I do and I will! The women that inspire me are the ones who have careers and children; why would I want to limit myself? I've always wanted to have children, and I would never give up that experience for a career. I want to have it all."[71]

Among all the theories that the media put out, very few reflected what Aniston's closest friends, and Aniston herself, viewed as the reasons that the marriage ended. When asked for the reason for the breakup, Aniston said simply, "I think—it changed. We both changed."[72]

Coping with Loss

While Pitt was happily globe trotting with Jolie, Aniston was left to play the part of the victim. Seen by the world as the wife who was left by her husband for another woman, Aniston was often the object of sympathy and even pity. Aniston hated the victim role, one she did not ask for and did not feel she deserved. She told *Vogue*:

> Don't feel sorry for me. Don't make me your victim. I don't want it. I'm so tired of being part of this sick, twisted Bermuda Triangle. As long as it's scandalous, it's a story. And that's kind of what it's been. It's just stupid. It's ridiculous. There's nothing to do about it. All I can do is go on and live my life. But like I've said before, these are human beings. And it's not a show and it's not an article and it's not a headline. It's real and it sucks.[73]

Soon after her divorce was announced, Aniston moved in to a small Malibu bungalow. There she worked through her feelings about Pitt and the end of her marriage. She depended on her friends a great deal, some of whom she had known for over twenty

Team Aniston

Soon after Brad Pitt and Jennifer Aniston separated, a trendy boutique in Los Angeles started selling baseball shirts inscribed with either "Team Aniston" or "Team Jolie." The Aniston shirts were hugely popular, outselling the Jolie shirts by twenty-five to one. It was not long before there was a three-month waiting list to get the sought-after shirts. Aniston herself was not thrilled about the shirts, saying: "I can see how that would be flattering, but that divide-and-conquer thing is stupid. It's just catty. I'm not catty."

Quoted in Josh Rottenberg, "What's Jennifer Aniston to Do?'" *Entertainment Weekly*, December 12, 2008, p. 24.

years. She also saw a therapist, which she has said was very helpful. "Am I lonely? Yes. Am I upset? Yes. Am I confused? Yes. Do I have my days when I've thrown a little pity party for myself? Absolutely," she told *Vanity Fair* a month before her divorce became final. "But I'm also doing really well, I've got an unbelievable support team, and I'm a tough cookie. . . . I feel very strong. I'm really proud of how I've conducted myself,"[74] she said.

Friends with Money

A few weeks after the couple announced their separation, Aniston started filming the ensemble film *Friends with Money*. Although the movie was a low-budget, independent film, Aniston was thrilled to have the opportunity to work with writer/director Nicole Holofcener. Holofcener knew she was taking a chance by casting Aniston, who was so well known for her role on *Friends*, but in the end, she felt that Aniston was right for the role regardless of what she had done in the past. In the movie, Aniston played Olivia, a single woman who quit her job as a teacher at a fancy private school. Now working as a housecleaner, Olivia stands out from her three friends, all of whom are wealthy, successful, and

Aniston started filming Friends with Money, *with Joan Cusack, left, and Catherine Keener, right, a few weeks after announcing her separation from Pitt.*

married. Aniston enjoyed working with Holofcener as well as the other women in the cast. She was especially excited about working with her longtime friend, actor Catherine Keener, who costarred with her in the movie.

While Aniston was filming *Friends with Money*, the public was watching the Aniston-Pitt-Jolie story unfold. The paparazzi followed her everywhere, including on location for movie shoots. Aniston's part required her to look somewhat drab and downtrodden. She wore very little makeup and old, baggy clothing, so when a photographer managed to catch her on film, she was often not at her best. "The paparazzi were getting pictures that were less than flattering to support the miserable person that they wanted to paint me as at the time,"[75] said Aniston. Although she was going through a difficult time, she managed to keep her sorrow to herself. "She was fine," said Holofcener. "She was completely composed and professional and seemed OK. She might not have been a barrel of monkeys because of what was happening, but she still had a really good vibe."[76]

Putting It in Perspective

No one could deny that the months leading up to the breakup with Pitt as well as the months after the divorce were hard on Aniston. Thanks to the paparazzi the details of her private life were splattered across headlines and discussed in living rooms and offices around the world. Often the tabloid stories were exaggerated or even completely untrue. In addition, the tabloids also kept close tabs on Pitt and Jolie. Aniston could not walk past a newsstand without seeing their smiling faces plastered below a headline raving about their latest adventure. Although the breakup and all the media coverage were not easy, Aniston realized they were not the worst things in the world, either. She put her breakup in perspective, saying: "The beauty of human resilience is that you do bounce back. And comparatively speaking to what people walk through, this is nothing. I haven't lost my home to some freak natural disaster. My son or my daughter is not in another country getting bombed. People just need to redirect their focus. It's like a little dark cloud that I'm just waiting to get out from under."[77]

Chapter 5

New Beginnings

By the time *Friends with Money* opened in January 2006, Aniston had learned that Jolie was pregnant with Pitt's baby and, further, that he had legally adopted her children, who now had the last names Jolie-Pitt. Although the news was painful, Aniston recovered quickly. She was, as always, able to turn to her friends for support, but for the first time in nearly ten years, she could also turn to her mother. Her breakup with Pitt had made her realize that she was ready to reconnect with Dow. "It's been really nice. It's crazy what, you know, your life kind of being turned upside down will lead you to. . . . For us it's . . . it was the time, and it was going to happen when it was supposed to happen. So this is good. It's baby steps,"[78] said Aniston.

Aniston was also doing well professionally. *Friends with Money* had been well received by critics, many of whom felt it was her best work since *The Good Girl*. In addition, over the summer she had filmed *The Break-Up*, which had not only helped her to get over her own breakup, but also launched her next relationship.

Movie-Making as Therapy

Aniston costarred in *The Break-Up* with actor/comedian Vince Vaughn. The movie is about a couple that breaks up but continues to live together in the condo they bought until it sells. Throughout the movie both parties seem to want to get back together but repeatedly hurt each other until both of their hearts are broken beyond repair.

One notable thing about the movie is how it correlated to Aniston's offscreen life. At least one movie critic credits the film's box office success to just that. David Edwards of the *UK Mirror* wrote: "Take two romantically-linked A-list stars, one of whom has just gone through a messy, highly-publicised split, and stick them in a film where they play a couple whose relationship is in meltdown. It doesn't matter if the movie's any good or not—this is a film that can't fail to make money."[79]

The movie did indeed make money—$118 million in the United States. However, for Aniston it was not about the movie's box office success, but rather about how working on the movie helped her to work through her own breakup with Pitt. She told *Elle* magazine: "This movie was fate. To be able to walk through

Vince Vaughn and Jennifer Aniston star in a scene from **The Break-Up** *in 2006. Aniston found working on the film to be cathartic.*

a movie called *The Break-Up*, about a person going through a breakup, while I'm actually going through a breakup?! How did that happen?! It's been cathartic. It's turned something into a fantastic experience. Not that divorce is fantastic, but I've never had more fun in a creative process."[80]

Aniston's costar Vince Vaughn was clearly a part of the fun she was having. During the shoot in Chicago in the summer of 2005, Aniston was seen having fun in public for the first time since announcing her separation at the start of the year. Although they were often part of a group, the two were frequently seen together, dancing, laughing, and even hugging. Aniston loved Vaughn's easygoing nature and the way he could always make her laugh. Vaughn was clearly equally fond of Aniston. "The thing with Jen is, she's so easy to feel drawn to," Vaughn said. "She's so genuine and warm, and she has a lightness, a classy ease about it all. You can see why people are so enamored. It's like she's stuffed with Elvis dust."[81]

As always the paparazzi followed them everywhere, insisting that they were romantically involved. At first they both denied it, saying that they were only good friends. Aniston often added that not only was Vaughn a good friend, he was also a loyal friend. However, it became harder to deny their romantic involvement when they were caught on camera locked in a passionate kiss.

Bouncing Back with Vince

As 2005 drew to a close, the tabloids continued to speculate about Aniston and Vaughn's relationship, though the couple themselves tried to keep it out of public view and did not attend large events together. Still, they were frequently seen snuggling up together in cozy restaurants and bars. Things got even more heated in April 2006, when a tabloid reported that the two were engaged and that talk show host Oprah Winfrey was planning to throw them an $8 million wedding. The report was believed by so many people that Aniston phoned in to Winfrey's show to deny the rumor publicly.

The couple continued to date through the summer and fall but broke up in December 2006. Both Aniston and Vaughn say the split was amicable and that they remain close friends.

Friends Reunion?

In February 2009 talk show host Ellen DeGeneres surprised Jennifer Aniston by taking her to the now-unused *Friends* Central Perk set and presenting her with a cake for her fortieth birthday. The set was still intact, and Aniston seemed genuinely happy to be there. While sitting on the couch, DeGeneres asked Aniston if she would consider a *Friends* reunion. Aniston was open to the idea, although she has said in the past that she would want it to be soon so that everyone would not be too old.

Several ideas have been tossed around by producers and cast members. Although a movie has been considered, Aniston, as well as costars Courteney Cox and Lisa Kudrow, would rather do a TV Thanksgiving special. However, the three male cast members are not interested in doing another show, so a *Friends* reunion seems unlikely, at least for now.

"I call Vince my defibrillator," Aniston said in a 2008 interview. "He literally brought me back to life. My first gasp of air was a *big laugh*! It was great. I love him. He's a bull in a china shop. He was lovely and fun and perfect for the time we had together. And I needed that. And it sort of ran its course."[82]

Taking a Break from the Big Screen

Professionally, Aniston was promoting *Friends with Money* and *The Break-Up* during the latter part of her relationship with Vaughn. She also tried her hand at directing. In *Room 10*, an eighteen-minute short sponsored by *Glamour* magazine, Aniston codirected actors Kris Kristofferson and Robin Wright Penn in a true story about a nurse and her terminally ill patient. According to Penn, as a director Aniston "was very loving and calm and knew what she wanted. She's not aggressive, meaning mean. But [she's] assertive with her vision, and making sure that everybody was in the team together."[83]

Jennifer Aniston wins the award for Favorite Female Movie Star at the 33rd Annual People's Choice Awards in Los Angeles.

Although she did not have a movie coming out in 2007, the year started well for Aniston. On January 9, exactly two years and two days after she and Pitt first announced their separation, Aniston won a People's Choice Award in the Favorite Female Movie Star category for *The Break-Up*. At the start of her acceptance speech, Aniston surprised and delighted the audience by saying, "Thank you for loving *The Break-Up*, I did."[84] Although she did not say it, her tone and facial expression made it clear that she was talking not just about the movie, but also about her breakup with Pitt. The audience responded with enthusiastic cheers and laughter.

That same month Aniston made *Forbes* magazine's Top 20 Richest Women in Entertainment. With a net worth of $110 million, Aniston came in at number ten, just behind Julia Roberts and Jennifer Lopez, but in front of the Olsen twins and Britney Spears.

A few months later, in March 2007, Aniston appeared as a guest star with Courteney Cox in the season finale of Cox's HBO show, *Dirt*. Aniston and Cox enjoyed working together again, and the episode was popular with audiences, not only because Aniston and Cox were reunited on the small screen, but also because Aniston played a lesbian magazine editor who planted a kiss on Cox during the episode.

Later that year, Aniston had a brief relationship with British male model Paul Sculfor. As with Vaughn, the two remain friends. However, her next relationship lasted significantly longer.

Ups and Downs with John

Jennifer Aniston first met singer/songwriter John Mayer at an Oscar party in February 2008. The two began dating in April. At thirty-nine, Aniston was eight years older than her new boyfriend. Over the next few months, the couple frequently traveled together and was spotted cuddling up in Miami, New York, and Mexico. In July Aniston joined Mayer on tour, hanging out backstage and reportedly getting along well with his crew and friends. However, just a month later Mayer broke up with Aniston. According to *People* reporter Laura Hahn, Mayer appeared "emotional, nervous and sad"[85] when he told her that he broke with Aniston because "people are different, people have different chemistry. I ended a relationship to be alone, because I don't want to waste somebody's time if something's not right."[86]

To many of Aniston's fans, the comment seemed cruel and unwarranted. However, Aniston did not hold it against him, saying: "It's funny when you hit a place in a relationship and you both realize [that] we maybe need to do something else, but you still really, really love each other. It's painful. There was no malicious intent. I deeply, deeply care about him; we talk, we adore one another. And that's where it is."[87]

The breakup only lasted about a month, and by October they were back together again. Aniston celebrated Mayer's thirty-first birthday with him later that month, and a few months later, Mayer was with Aniston for her fortieth in February. Mayer even wrote a special song for the occasion. They attended the 2009 Oscars together in late February, happily posing together on the red carpet. However, in mid-March, the couple surprised everyone by breaking up again. Tabloids claimed that Aniston broke up with Mayer after discovering he was spending hours updating his status on Twitter, a popular social networking Internet site, while claiming he was too busy at work to return her phone calls.

Toward the end of her relationship with Mayer, Aniston filmed *Management*, in which she played a traveling saleswoman. The movie did poorly with critics and had a poor showing at the box office, not even clearing the $1 million mark. She received much better marks for her guest appearance on Tina Fey's hit TV sitcom, *30 Rock*, in November 2008. Although audiences enjoyed seeing Aniston on the small screen, it would not be long before they would get the chance to see her in another big-screen blockbuster.

Marley and Me

Marley and Me was released on December 25, 2008. The movie made $14.75 million on its opening day; a box office record for movies opening on Christmas Day. By the end of its run, the movie had made over $143 million. Aniston costarred in the movie with comedic actor Owen Wilson and a yellow Labrador

Aniston and musician John Mayer met at an Oscar party in 2008. The relationship lasted less than a year.

Aniston and Her Dogs

It is not surprising that Jennifer Aniston got along well with the dogs on the *Marley and Me* set. She loves dogs and in June 2009 was voted the celebrity people would trust most with their pets on a Paw Nation online poll. Aniston has owned several dogs over the years and currently has two dogs, Norman and Dolly.

Norman is a Welsh corgi–terrier mix, now thirteen years old. Aniston adopted Norman as a puppy while she was working on *Friends*. He had been trained for work in movies and on TV but had earned a reputation for being lazy. Aniston adores Norman and considers him to be "a person in a dog suit."

Aniston adopted Dolly as a puppy in 2006. Dolly is a white German shepherd that Aniston thought would make a good guard dog. When she was a puppy, Dolly chewed up shoes and expensive rugs in Aniston's house. Aniston jokes that she almost sent her back to the pound for that.

Aniston values the companionship of her dogs a great deal. She frequently walks them on the beach and often takes Norman with her on location when filming movies.

Quoted in Julie Jordon, "Year End 2008, Jennifer Aniston," *People*, December 29, 2008, p. 65.

retriever. Actually, the retriever, Marley, was played by twenty-two different dogs. Based on the 2005 best-selling memoir by newspaper columnist John Grogan, the movie is a true story about Grogan, his wife, and their lovable but troublesome dog. Spanning fifteen years, the movie is filled with plenty of humorous dog scenes, but also explores the joys and challenges of career and family life.

Aniston worked well with Wilson as well as the dogs, though there were some challenges. While they were filming dog scenes, the trainers were commanding the dogs, so the actors had to perform with that distracting noise in the background. However, the hardest part for Aniston was the end of the shoot, when she had to say good-bye to the dogs. In fact, she nearly adopted one of the puppies. "I was surprisingly quite emotional," said Aniston. "I really bonded with the dogs. We had babies, puppies, children, adult dogs, old dogs and we all had a ball while shooting."[88]

In addition to working with dogs for the first time, Aniston was also playing a real person for the first time, rather than a fictional character. Both Aniston and Wilson knew they needed to portray

Jennifer Aniston and Owen Wilson star in a scene from the film Marley and Me *in 2008. For the film, Aniston starred with dogs for the first time and she also played a real person for the first time.*

their characters in ways that were faithful to the book. "It was something that was extremely important to us because this book has such an audience and such a fan base and these are two people that are actually here on the planet and you want to honor their story,"[89] said Aniston. For their part, both Grogan and his wife were thrilled with the casting and even visited the set a few times.

Aniston's next movie, the romantic comedy *He's Just Not That Into You*, came out in February 2009, just in time for Valentine's Day. In this ensemble film Aniston played one of several loosely connected women, all in the midst of relationship difficulties. The movie features a star-studded cast, including Drew Barrymore, Scarlett Johansson, and Jennifer Connelly. In the movie, Aniston leaves her boyfriend of seven years, played by Ben Affleck, because although he is committed to her, he will not marry her. The movie received mixed reviews, though some critics felt that Aniston's performance stood out. "Surprisingly, Affleck and Aniston create the two most appealing people in the movie—both actors let their maturity show in unexpected ways,"[90] noted *Boston Globe* film critic Ty Burr.

At Home with Aniston

Although a great deal of her time has been spent shooting movies and globe trotting with friends and romantic partners, Aniston is in many ways a homebody at heart. She values her time at home and has worked hard to create a sanctuary for herself and her two beloved dogs, Norman and Dolly.

In October 2006 Aniston bought a new home for $15 million in Beverly Hills. The house was designed in the early 1970s by renowned architect Hal Levitt and is just minutes away from Courteney Cox's home. The entire 9,000 square feet (836 sq. m) of the home is located on one floor. The house has six bedrooms and seven bathrooms. Originally, Aniston had planned a four-month renovation project; however, the house was found to have structural problems, causing the renovations to take nearly two years. Among other things, the finished house has solar panels, an indoor/outdoor fireplace, a Japanese soaking tub, and a custom pool with a waterfall running its entire length. Aniston consulted

Aniston Pokes Fun at Her Own Movie Titles

On June 12, 2009, Jennifer Aniston was presented with the prestigious Crystal Award at the Women in Films Lucy and Crystal Awards ceremony. In her acceptance speech, Aniston took a humorous approach, saying:

> I'm trying to be more careful than I have been in the past about the titles of movies I choose to be in. It's funny—I kind of noticed a few years ago, there seems to be a strange parallel between the movies I'm doing and my life off-screen. It started with "The Good Girl," then of course "Rumor Has It," followed by "Derailed." Then there was "The Break Up." If any of you have a project entitled "Everlasting Love with a Stable Adult Male" I'm at table 6 and my agents are at table 12!

Quoted in *Access Hollywood,* "Jennifer Aniston Looks for 'Everlasting Love' at Lucy and Crystal Awards," June 13, 2009. www.accesshollywood.com/jennifer-aniston-looks-for-everlasting-love-at-crystal-and-lucy-awards_article_19220.

Jennifer Aniston received a Crystal Award at the Women in Films Lucy and Crystal Awards ceremony on June 12, 2009. The speech she gave was humorous and poked fun at her movie titles.

an interior decorator to help with the inside, which is decorated in an Indonesian style. "I wanted to have that feeling that when you walked in you were able to throw your feet up and just be peaceful. But I also wanted it to feel . . . sexy,"[91] says Aniston.

Aniston's "sexy" house is a perfect match for her sexy body. According to *GQ* reporter Mark Kirby: "Jen looks at least as young, if not younger, than she did during her *Friends* days, this despite her looming fortieth birthday. She looks *better*, too—fit and sun kissed as always, but somehow in greater possession of herself and seemingly at ease with her age."[92] Readers can see for themselves, as Aniston posed nearly nude for the magazine shortly before her fortieth birthday.

Movies, Movies, and More Movies

In addition to *He's Just Not That Into You*, Aniston starred in another 2009 movie, *Love Happens*. The romantic drama is about a widower who gives self-help seminars after writing a book about loss. While in Seattle he falls for a florist, who helps him to realize that he is not truly over his loss.

Aniston had two very different movies come out in 2010. In *The Baster* Aniston played a single woman who gets pregnant using artificial insemination only to discover years later that the baby's father may not be who she thinks he is. In contrast, *The Bounty* is an action movie about a bounty hunter who discovers that his next target is his wife.

Aniston shows no signs of slowing down in the coming years. In addition to acting, she is also planning to produce. Although Pitt got Plan B when they divorced, Aniston and longtime friend Kristin Hahn started a new production company called Echo Films in 2008. The company's emphasis is on telling real-life stories, and many of their projects are based on best-selling books or true stories. "We're drawn to stories about people finding their voice and finding their way because they help us as listeners and viewers do what we feel we're all trying to do, which is making sense of our lives through the stories of others," Aniston said. "That's why we chose the name Echo, to echo back an idea, a challenge, something that resonates through all of us."[93]

Jennifer Aniston and Gerard Butler appear on location in Brooklyn, New York, filming The Bounty, *due in theaters in 2010.*

Echo has several movies in development, most of which will star Aniston. *The Divorce* and *Getting Rid of Matthew* are both based on best-selling books and focus on relationship issues. *Counter Clockwise* and *Chemistry* both have their base in social psychology. *Counter Clockwise* is about a real-life psychological experiment designed to slow the aging process, and *Chemistry* explores the brain connection between romantic love and obsessive compulsive disorder. *Love, Todd*, which will not star Aniston, is about an aging tennis pro who coaches a promising young athlete. However, the project Aniston is most excited about is a musical set in the 1940s.

The Goree Girls is based on a true story about a group of eight inmates in a Texas prison who formed the first all-female country-and-western band in the United States. Although the members of the band did not have musical backgrounds and were in prison, they became hugely popular with Fort Worth radio listeners. Echo is working with DreamWorks to produce the film that will also feature Scottish actor Gerard Butler. Already, movie buffs are wondering if Aniston will be a convincing prison inmate and, more importantly, if she can sing.

Right Where She's Supposed to Be

For most of her adult life, Aniston has been in the spotlight. She gained almost instant fame during the first season of *Friends*, becoming one of television's favorite stars. She successfully made the jump from the small screen to the big one, making over twenty movies, including several blockbusters. With a salary of $8 million per movie, she is one of Hollywood's highest paid actresses.

Not only has the public watched Aniston on TV and in the movies, but it has also eagerly watched, discussed, and judged her real-life successes and failures. Details of her seemingly ideal marriage to Brad Pitt and painful divorce a few years later often made headlines, as well as her romantic relationships after Pitt. Often, the public sentiment was to feel sorry for this extraordinarily beautiful, wealthy, and successful actor. Aniston recently told *Vogue* why no one should feel sorry for her:

> This whole "Poor lonely Jen" thing, this idea that I'm so unlucky in love? I actually feel I've been *unbelievably* lucky in love. Just because at this stage my life doesn't have the traditional framework to it—the husband and the two kids and the house in Connecticut—it's *mine*. It's my experience. And if you don't like the way it looks, then stop looking at it! Because I feel good. I don't feel like I'm supposed to be any further along or somewhere that I'm not. I'm right where I'm supposed to be.[94]

Chapter 1: A Rocky Beginning

1. Nancy Aniston, *From Mother and Daughter to Friends: A Memoir*. Amherst, NY: Prometheus, 1999, p. 44.
2. Aniston, *From Mother and Daughter to Friends*, p. 156.
3. Quoted in Nancy Collins, "Life's Never Been Better," *Rolling Stone*, March 1999, p. 58.
4. Quoted in Rich Cohen, "The Girl Friend," *Rolling Stone*, March 2, 1996. www.rollingstone.com/news/story/5938503/the_girl_friend.
5. Quoted in *Access Hollywood*, "Access Archives: Jennifer Aniston," video. www.accesshollywood.com/access-archives-jennifer-aniston_video_136563.
6. Quoted in Cal Fussman, "A Woman We Love: Jennifer Aniston," *Esquire*, October 2002, p. 112.
7. Quoted in Fussman, "A Woman We Love," p. 112.
8. Quoted in Marlo Thomas and Friends, *The Right Words at the Right Time*. New York: Atria, 2002, p. 11.
9. Quoted in Collins, "Life's Never Been Better," p. 58.
10. Quoted in Thomas and Friends, *The Right Words at the Right Time*, p. 12.
11. Quoted in Cohen, "The Girl Friend."
12. Quoted in Sean Smith, *Jennifer: The Unauthorized Biography*. London: Pan, 2007, p. 167.
13. Quoted in Leslie Bennetts, "Deconstructing Jennifer," *Vanity Fair*, May 2001, p. 162.
14. Quoted in Collins, "Life's Never Been Better," p. 59.
15. Marc Savlov, "Leprechaun," *Austin Chronicle*, January 15, 1993. www.austinchronicle.com/gyrobase/Calendar/Film?Film=oid%3A139314.
16. Quoted in *People*, "Most Beautiful First Timers," May 10, 1999, p. 192.

Chapter 2: *Friends Like Us*

17. Quoted in Cohen, "The Girl Friend."

18. Marta Kauffman and David Crane, "The Pilot," *Friends*, NBC, September 22, 1994.
19. Quoted in Smith, *Jennifer*, p. 163.
20. Quoted in David Wild, *Friends ... 'til the End*. New York: Time Inc. Home Entertainment, 2004, p. 10.
21. Quoted in Wild, *Friends . . . 'til the End*, p. 24.
22. Quoted in Bennetts, "Deconstructing Jennifer," p. 162.
23. Quoted in Wild, *Friends . . . 'til the End*, p. 61.
24. Quoted in Wild, *Friends . . . 'til the End*, p. 58.
25. Quoted in Craig Tomashoff, "The Joy of Six," *People,* April 17, 1995, p. 80.
26. Quoted in Wild, *Friends . . . 'til the End*, p. 26.
27. Quoted in Douglas Thompson, "Jennifer Aniston Interview," Douglas Thompson: Biographer, Writer, Journalist. www .dougiethompson.com/JenniferAniston_page1.htm.
28. Quoted in Wild, *Friends . . . 'til the End*, p. 10.
29. Quoted in Wild, *Friends . . . 'til the End*, p. 85.
30. Quoted in Gayle Jo Carter, "Jennifer Aniston—on Her Own," *USA Weekend*, July 25, 1997. www.usaweekend.com/97_issues /970727/970727cov_aniston.html.
31. Quoted in Academy of Television Arts and Sciences, "54th Annual Primetime Emmy Awards," NBC, September 22, 2002.
32. Ruthe Stein, "Film Review—Aniston Tries to Be More than Friends in 'Perfect,'" *San Francisco Chronicle*, August 1, 1997. www.sfgate.com/cgi-bin/article.cgi?f=/c/a/1997/08/01/ DD10559.DTL.
33. Quoted in Carter, "Jennifer Aniston—on Her Own."

Chapter 3: Hollywood's Golden Couple

34. Quoted in Jonathan Van Meter, "A Profile in Courage," *Vogue*, April 2006, p. 410.
35. Quoted in Carter, "Jennifer Aniston—on Her Own."
36. Quoted in *People*, "Scoop," November 16, 1998, p. 10.
37. Quoted in Collins, "Life's Never Been Better," p. 59.
38. Quoted in Chris Heath, "The Unbearable Bradness of Being," *Rolling Stone*, October 28, 1999, p. 68.
39. Quoted in Bennetts, "Deconstructing Jennifer," p. 162.

40. Quoted in Anne-Marie O'Neill, "Isn't It Romantic?" *People*, August 14, 2000, p. 116.
41. Quoted in O'Neill, "Isn't It Romantic?" p. 116.
42. Quoted in O'Neill, "Isn't It Romantic?" p. 116.
43. Quoted in Bennetts, "Deconstructing Jennifer," p. 162.
44. Quoted in Bennetts, "Deconstructing Jennifer," p. 162.
45. Quoted in Karen S. Schneider, "As Good as It Gets," *People*, August 26, 2002, p. 86.
46. Quoted in Alex Tresniowski, "Jennifer Aniston: The 50 Most Beautiful People," *People*, May 10, 2004, p. 82.
47. Craig Marine, "Lots of Room for Laughs in Office Space," *San Francisco Examiner*, February 19, 1999. www.sfgate.com/cgi bin/article.cgi?f=/e/a/1999/02/19/WEEKEND13550.dtl.
48. Quoted in *The Good Girl*, "Commentary," DVD, directed by Miguel Arteta. Los Angeles: 20th Century Fox, 2003.
49. Mark Sells, "The Good Girl," The Reel Deal. www.oregonherald .com/reviews/mark-sells/reviews/goodgirl.html.
50. Quoted in Bennetts, "Deconstructing Jennifer," p. 162.
51. Quoted in *Breaking News*, "Jennifer Aniston Wants to Quit and Start a Family." http://archives.tcm.ie/breakingnews/2002/ 12/17/story81017.asp.
52. Andrew O'Hehir, "Bruce Almighty," Salon.com. http://dir.salon .com/story/ent/movies/review/2003/05/23/bruce/index.html? CP=IMD&DN=110.
53. Quoted in Jeff Otto, "An Interview with Jennifer Aniston and Ben Stiller," IGN Movies, January 14, 2004. http://movies.ign .com/articles/463/463173p1.html.
54. David Edelstein, "Poop Goes the Weasel," *Slate*, January 15, 2004. www.slate.com/id/2092179.

Chapter 4: Time for Good-Byes

55. Quoted in MSNBC, "Aniston 'Picking Up Pieces' After Split with Pitt," August 2, 2005. www.msnbc.msn.com/id/8801720.
56. Quoted in Michelle Tauber and Chris Struss, "He Said, She Said," *People*, June 20, 2005, p. 67.
57. Quoted in Tresniowski, "Jennifer Aniston," p. 82.
58. Quoted in Leslie Bennetts, "The Unsinkable Jennifer Aniston," *Vanity Fair*, September 2005, p. 393.

59. Quoted in *Dateline*, "A Farewell to Friends," NBC, May 5, 2004.
60. Quoted in Wild, *Friends … 'til the End*, p. 258.
61. Quoted in *People*, "Two on the Town," January 26, 2004, p. 50.
62. Robert Bianco, "Rachel Stays, so 'Friends' Are Able to Leave Together," *USA Today*, May 7, 2004, p. 10A.
63. Meghan Keane, "Where Have You Gone, Mrs. Robinson?" *New York Sun*, December 23, 2005. www.nysun.com/arts/where-have-you-gone-mrs-robinson/24925.
64. William Arnold, "'Rumor Has It . . . ': Aniston Gets a Nice Break," *Seattle Post Intelligencer*, December 25, 2005. www.seattlepi.com/movies/253104_rumor23q.html.
65. Quoted in Van Meter, "A Profile in Courage," p. 409.
66. Quoted in Holly Milea, "The Better Girl," *Elle*, October 3, 2005. www.elle.com/Entertainment/Cover-Shoots/The-Better-Girl/Jennifer-Aniston.
67. Quoted in Van Meter, "A Profile in Courage, p. 409.
68. Quoted in *People*, "Jennifer Aniston and Brad Pitt Separate," January 7, 2005. www.people.com/people/article/0,,1015778,00.html.
69. Quoted in Bennetts, "The Unsinkable Jennifer Aniston," p. 390.
70. Quoted in Bennetts, "The Unsinkable Jennifer Aniston," p. 392.
71. Quoted in Bennetts, "The Unsinkable Jennifer Aniston," p. 391.
72. Quoted in Bennetts, "The Unsinkable Jennifer Aniston," p. 393.
73. Quoted in Van Meter, "A Profile in Courage," p. 378.
74. Quoted in Bennetts, "The Unsinkable Jennifer Aniston," p. 391.
75. Quoted in Van Meter, "A Profile in Courage," p. 410.
76. Quoted in Van Meter, "A Profile in Courage," p. 410.
77. Quoted in Van Meter, "A Profile in Courage," p. 409.

Chapter 5: New Beginnings

78. Quoted in *Good Morning America*, "Jennifer Aniston Finds Peace After Brad," ABC News, November 8, 2005. http://abcnews.go.com/GMA/story?id=1289634.
79. David Edwards, "The Break-Up," *Daily Mirror*, July 21, 2006. www.mirror.co.uk/tm_objectid=17411954&method=full&siteid=115875&headline=the-break-up-name_page.html.
80. Quoted in Milea, "The Better Girl."

81. Quoted in Milea, "The Better Girl."

82. Quoted in Jonathan Van Meter, "Prime Time," *Vogue,* December 2008, p. 312.

83. Quoted in Fox News, "Jennifer Aniston Makes Directing Debut with 'Room 10,'" October 17, 2006. www.foxnews.com/story/0,2933,221741,00.html.

84. Quoted in CBS, "33rd Annual People's Choice Awards," January 9, 2007.

85. Laura Hahn, "John on Breakup with Jen: There Was No Lying, No Cheating," *People,* August 16, 2008. www.people.com/people/article/0,,20219799,00.html.

86. Quoted in Hahn, "John on Breakup with Jen."

87. Quoted in Van Meter, "Prime Time," p. 312.

88. Quoted in Robin Bansal, "Marley & Me About Marriage, Career . . . and a Dog," Indo-Asian News Service, February 5, 2009. www.hindustantimes.com/StoryPage/StoryPage.aspx?id=5f8099e5-0e8c-4640-85f5-287ede97bfba.

89. Quoted in Paul Fischer, "Jennifer Aniston Marley and Me Interview," Girl.com. www.girl.com.au/jennifer-aniston-marley-and-me-interview.htm.

90. Ty Burr, "When Will She Be Loved?" *Boston Globe*, February 6, 2009. www.boston.com/movies/display?display=movie&id=10981.

91. Quoted in Van Meter, "Prime Time," p. 306.

92. Mark Kirby, "Lordy, Lordy, This Woman Is 40," *GQ,* January 2009, p. 60.

93. Quoted in Michael Fleming, "Jennifer Aniston Forms Echo Films," *Variety*, March 31, 2008. www.variety.com/article/VR1117983220.html?categoryid=13&cs=1.

94. Quoted in Van Meter, "Prime Time," p. 308.

1969
Jennifer Joanne Aniston is born on February 11 in Sherman Oaks, California.

1987
Aniston graduates from the Fiorello H. LaGuardia High School of Music & Art and Performing Arts.

1990
Aniston appears in the made-for-TV movie *Camp Cucamonga* as well as the short-lived sitcoms *Molloy* and *Ferris Bueller*.

1993
Aniston stars in her first major motion picture, *Leprechaun*.

1994
Aniston lands the role of Rachel Green on the sitcom *Friends*; midway through the first season, she gets her hair cut in a bouncy shag that is dubbed the "the Rachel" and becomes one of the most popular hairstyles of all time.

1996
Aniston cuts off all contact with her mother, Nancy Dow, after Dow gives an unflattering interview to a TV tabloid show.

2000
Aniston marries actor Brad Pitt in an elaborate million-dollar wedding on July 29, 2000.

2001
Aniston wins the first of four consecutive People's Choice Awards for her work on *Friends*; she and Pitt purchase a 10,000-square-foot (929 sq. m) mansion in Beverly Hills and begin a two-year renovation.

2002
Aniston wins an Emmy Award for Outstanding Lead Actress in a Comedy Series for *Friends*; plays downtrodden Justine in the

movie *The Good Girl* and is praised by critics for finally breaking free of her Rachel Green persona.

2003

Forbes magazine ranks Aniston as number one its list of the 100 Top Celebrities; Aniston wins a Golden Globe Award for her work on *Friends*; stars with comedic actor Jim Carrey in the blockbuster hit *Bruce Almighty*.

2004

The final episode of *Friends* is filmed, completing its run of ten years.

2005

Aniston and Pitt issue a joint statement declaring that they are separating on January 7, 2005; Aniston files for divorce on March 25, and the divorce becomes final on October 2; Aniston rekindles her relationship with her estranged mother.

2006

Aniston stars in *The Break-Up* opposite actor Vince Vaughn, and the two begin dating; Aniston purchases a house in Beverly Hills for $13.5 million.

2008

Aniston appears with Owen Wilson in *Marley and Me*; founds Echo Films with longtime friend Kristin Hahn.

For More Information

Books

John Grogan, *Marley: A Dog Like No Other*. New York: Harper-Collins, 2008. Grogan adapts *Marley and Me* for younger readers in this delightful book that tells the story of Marley and his family. Includes pictures of the real Marley.

Lauren Johnson, *Friends: The Official Trivia Guide*. New York: Penguin, 2004. Hundred of trivia questions fill the pages of this book, along with fun facts, photos, and sidebars about various aspects of the show.

Sarah Marshall, *Jennifer Aniston: The Biography of Hollywood's Sweetheart*. London: John Blake, 2007. This biography covers the major events of Aniston's childhood, career, and personal life.

David Wild, *Friends . . . 'til the End*. New York: Time Inc. Home Entertainment, 2004. This authorized commemorative book celebrates the ten years of *Friends* and includes episode guides for every season, interviews with the cast members and producers, as well as plenty of quotes and pictures from the show.

Periodical

Julie Jordon, "Year End 2008 Jennifer Aniston," *People*, December 29, 2008.

Web Sites

Crazy for Friends (www.livesinabox.com/friends). Everything about the TV show *Friends* can be found on this fan site, including pictures, trivia, episode details, and scripts.

Jennifer Aniston, Internet Movie Database (www.imdb.com/name/nm0000098/filmotype). This site has an updated filmography of Aniston's work as well as pictures, a list of awards she has won, and a brief biography.

People (www.people.com/people). A wealth of articles about Aniston as well as other celebrities can be found on this site.

Picture Credits

Cover image: © Frank Trapper/Corbis
Brian Ach/WireImage/Getty Images, 83
AP Images, 10, 34, 43, 45, 62, 68, 74, 77
CBS Photo Archive/Getty Images, 15
L. Cohen/WireImage/Getty Images, 54
Marion Curtis/DMI/Time Life Pictures/Getty Images, 14
Paul Drinkwater/NBCU Photo Bank via AP Images, 29, 58–59
Everett Collection, 25
FM/FilmMagic/Getty Images, 19
Fox 2000 Pictures/The Kobal Collection, 79
Alice S. Hall/NBCU Photo Bank via AP Images, 32
Kevin Mazur/WireImage/Getty Images, 31
© Melissa Moseley/SMPSP/Warner Bros/Bureau L.A.
   Collection/Corbis, 63
NBCU Photo Bank via AP Images, 23
Lucy Nicholson/AFP/Getty Images, 38
© Photos 12/Alamy, 51
Ron Galella, Ltd./WireImage/Getty Images, 27
Michael Sanville/WireImage/Getty Images, 46
John Shearer/WireImage/Getty Images, 81
Jim Smeal/WireImage/Getty Images, 37
Mirek Towski/DMI/Time Life Pictures/Getty Images, 17
Yoshikazu Tsuno/AFP/Getty Images, 65
20th Century Fox/The Kobal Collection, 40, 57
Universal/The Kobal Collection/Moseley, Melissa, 71
© Warner Bros./Courtesy: Everett Collection, 49

About the Author

Rachel Lynette has written more than sixty books for children of all ages as well as resource materials for teachers. She lives in the Seattle area with her two delightful children, David and Lucy, and a cat named Cosette. When she is not writing, she enjoys spending time with her family and friends, traveling, reading, drawing, crocheting colorful hats, biking, and sailing.